Edy Brunner

Edy Brunner

Conceptualist
Artist
Photographer
Designer

Edited by Axel Wendelberger

With texts by
Franz Hohler, Willy Rotzler and Axel Wendelberger

EDITION STEMMLE

Contents

Many facets – one image: Edy Brunner the generalist

An explosion of ideas, a fireworks of artistic creativity – where does one begin to describe an artist whose work ranges from concept art to kinetic art, from serial art to environments, taking in environmental design, art for public spaces, interior decor, exhibition design, and even photography, on the way? Any attempt to classify the artist Edy Brunner invariably means misconstruing his artistic intention right from the start. After all, what is the driving force behind a man whose creative energy pushes him to such a variety of experiments, creating utterly sensational works in every field he turns to, only to head off in a new direction again and address completely different issues? Given an oeuvre of such scope and diversity, is it possible to develop a distinctive and clearly legible personal style?

These are the questions that inevitably crop up in any reflection on the work of this highly versatile artist, born in Bern in 1943. If there is one thing that cannot be found in his oeuvre, it is an easy answer. His work seduces us, drawing us into his conceptual approach, calling on us to exercise our own creative intellectual faculties. Edy Brunner frequently pinpoints remarkable contextual synchronicities in his immediate environment, triggering a chain of associations that culminates in the visualisation of a certain underlying idea. In doing so, the fitting transposition of the concept in question is more important to him than the medium through which he expresses it. He always chooses whatever is appropriate.

Edy Brunner has been working as an artist for 30 years. Never having undergone any specific training in the form of an academic course of study, he may be regarded as self-taught. This fact has ensured an invariably unconventional approach to artistic media throughout his career. Brunner has always been able to sum up even the most complex of situations and contexts very quickly indeed. Willy Rotzler has described this as his "gift of seeing". It is Brunner's special talent and the fount of all his creative expression. Whether he works with everyday objects such as sockets, screws or artificial flowers, creating objects of subtlety and wit, whether he breaks processes down into individual photographic images and documents them in the form of large tableaus, whether he constructs a kinetic fountain out of huge rough-hewn boulders in front of a major insurance company, designs a trade fair stand in the form of an enormous granite cube for a plastics manufacturer, or captures urban landscapes with a panorama camera, behind it all there is invariably a carefully considered concept that permits aspects of everyday life – situations, processes, objects, materials – to appear in an aesthetically determined light.

Edy Brunner's creative intention is to be elucidated here by way of example of his most significant works. As he himself rejects all that is definitive and final, this publication can give no conclusive survey of this restless artist. The very fact that it is divided into chapters on concept and art, photography and

design, tends to limit our way of seeing, for Brunner has created many of his works simultaneously and in parallel. Nevertheless, this method does reveal certain steps and changes in his development. Brunner's approach to his environment becomes evident in many ways: critical, but not patronising. The fact that he has never adopted a "hallmark" makes him seem suspect to the art market, and at the same time underlines the credibility of his message to us.

Axel Wendelberger
Zurich, April 1995

Edy Brunner or the gift of seeing

My approach to art has always involved searching for answers to questions as to art's essential nature. The answers, originally as complex as the issue itself, have become ever simpler over the years. Today I would say that the deciding factor for an artist is his ability to see. This alone differentiates him from the non-artist. Everything needed to produce a work of art can be acquired: the structural tools of form and color, artistic techniques, manual skill with materials. But being able to see is a gift.

I want to make it clear what I mean: in addition to outward seeing, to heightened perception of the phenomena around us, there is also an inward seeing which is just as important. Introspection and extraspection are complementary forms of this one ability to see.

I have always admired Edy Brunner for how he sees and what he sees – more, at any rate, and differently than most do. Seeing is for him an existential need, but at the same time a pleasurable, a sensual capacity. When he sees, ideas or even chains of ideas are triggered by association – ideas of definition, of intervention, of change and transformation, of concretization, of connection, of alienation. Tireless and inexhaustible idea men like Edy Brunner usually stop with producing one surprising, stimulating idea or chain of ideas after another. "Live in your head" was the challenge Harald Szeeman made in his 1969 exhibition in the Kunsthalle Bern entitled "When Attitudes Become Form". The exhibition was a decisive influence on Edy Brunner's generation, by no means only in Bern.

For all his declared belief in creative seeing and in mental processing, connecting and transforming of visual impressions, Edy Brunner is driven again and again to shape and form what he sees, and the ideas developed out of what he sees. He is not only a concept artist but also a producer of works of art. However: since ideas in all their rich variety are his central interest, he cannot restrict himself to any single medium. He is no specialist – a generalist rather, example of a type of artist not possible before our time, who makes good use of art's expansion and of the new boundlessness of the arts. Just a summary of Edy Brunner's creative works and activities might convey the impression of a man trying to have his cake and eat it many times over.

Such an impression would be false. It is true that Edy Brunner has, over the past two decades, taken up and let go an almost inconceivable variety of projects. But all are nothing other than different facets of one and the same basic ability: the gift of seeing and the ability to visualize, appropriately and compellingly, the ideas developed out of what is seen.

This is true for the object artist, who assembles prefabricated forms and parts to develop surprisingly new things. It is true for the experimenter with multiples, who has paced off its possibilities as a new art form. It is true for the environmental

designer, active since the early seventies, who has given a look and a climate worth living in to public squares, playgrounds, and gardens. It is true for the environmental sculptor, who combines materials, mechanical laws, and forces of nature into imposing monumental sculptures. Seeing, thinking, and expression in form are combined perhaps most clearly in the photographic works and photo-experiments of Edy Brunner. I am thinking of the fascinating series of documentary photographs, like the 1,144 snapshots of a ride through the Gotthard Tunnel mounted as one picture. They have offered us new perspectives on reality as it unfolds in real time.

Now Edy Brunner surprises us with a series of mostly quiet, indeed empty wide-angle pictures of a strangeness, beauty, and formal power as enchanting as they are mysterious. Were they not unmistakeably images or motifs from the real world, from our world, captured by the camera, it would be tempting to describe them as relicts of another world, as traces of a dream or a world of art. These gentle or emphatic visual poems contain so much of the substance of nature, as of man-made reality, that creating stories or poetry to go with them is a natural next step.

Of course, most of Edy Brunner's scenes are not just around the corner. They had to be discovered over time, on many trips to many countries, and seen in all their oddness or their beauty. Their values – their stillness, infinity, desertedness, contradiction, their enigmatic quality, the formal perfection of their motifs – were so strong that Edy Brunner could dispense with any photographic manipulation. The only "trick" used by this alert observer is the extremely wide format, not achieved by cropping: a breadth that exceeds our normal angle of vision. This "different view" of reality is the source of at least some of the powerful effect of these pictures.

The wide-angle photographs here presented as realities by a seer, that is an artist, remind of the words of Georges Braque, the painter: "Art exists to nourish unease; science creates certainty."

Willy Rotzler

Concept and Art

Concept and Art

Edy Brunner has never sought formal multiplicity. He did not undergo the kind of academic training that persuades artists to accept the importance of a distinctive signature. This has allowed him to approach artistic media with fresh eyes, unburdened by any sense of obligation to specialize in one particular field. This fact permeates his entire oeuvre. In spite of the wealth of experience he has gained in 30 years of creative work, he has maintained this natural impartiality right up to the present day.

For all the variety in Bunner's oeuvre, there are nevertheless a number of obvious constants which lend his works their distinctive character. Edy Brunner invariably works with stimulating ideas and thought processes; he does not merely play with form. For him, the starting point of the artistic conception of a work is a question of mind over matter. In other words, the act of creating a work of art is an intellectual process: visualizing a concept is more important to him than executing a work in a certain medium. In this sense, Edy Brunner is a pure conceptualist. After all, whether or not an idea is actually executed has no bearing whatsoever on its quality.

If there is any one genre to which Edy Brunner feels particularly attracted, then it is concrete art. Although he has never been its exponent, it possesses a formal stringency that has much in common with his approach. Reducing both the thought and the medium to the absolute minimum is a distinctive feature of all Brunner's works. Such creative discipline guarantees a high degree of efficiency. For Brunner, it would be unthinkable to develop an idea without any bearing on the tangibly perceptible environment. Often, he takes as his starting point everyday items or found materials such as sockets, screws, roadblock signs, artificial flowers and stones, which he then alienates and processes in order to visualize the respective concept. Nor does he regard contract assignments as restrictive; in fact he is highly productive when working in that field of tension between the client's brief and his own idea. His experience in the field of exhibition design since the 70s reflects this clearly; it is a field in which contract assignments and observation of specifications form the basis of his work.

Nevertheless, formal discipline is not an end in itself for Brunner. It merely creates the necessary counterpoint to offset his own rampant creativity. A playful approach to ideas and thoughts is the wellspring of this artist's unconventional output. Given the fact that his playful intellect is not satisfied with definitive states, but invariably seeks new slants and angles, new ways of using existing objects, even exploring elements of insecurity or chaos, it is hardly surprising to find that Brunner frequently uses familiar materials and techniques in unusual ways. He often does so with an inimitable sense of humour, as is evident in his multiple of artificial flowers to be used as permanently circulating gifts, in his molecular fountain of tangled

pipes for a pharmaceutical company, or in the mirror he floated on the river Limmat in Zurich, creating a pun on the German word for water level – *Wasserspiegel* – which, literally translated, also means "water mirror". Such conceptual humour has its roots in the world of Marcel Duchamp, whose work Brunner admires.

Visualizing concepts is not only an intellectual technique, but the clearest form of expression of Brunner's approach. It is, as it were, his stylistic hallmark. With few early exceptions, there has been no abstract, purely formal design concept in his work. Sensory experiences are invariably the starting point, while the actual execution of an idea, the work of art, makes an intellectual process tangible again. In this way, he succeeds in making the spectator reflect on his works, in what is invariably a highly pleasurable intellectual experience.

Metre Rule Works

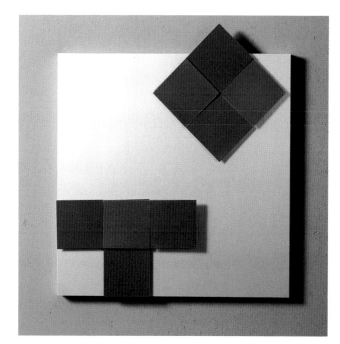

1966/67

10-part metre rule (100 cm), wood,
aluminium, anodized in various colours, mobile
50 x 50 cm

Edy Brunner made his first forays into the world of experimental art as an employee of the Basel-based advertising agency GGK (Gerstner, Gredinger & Kutter), where the intellectual atmosphere captured his imagination, inspiring him to work freely. Karl Gerstner, with his concrete and mobile works, was an important role model. In 1966/67 Brunner created his first serial and mobile works using simple media and materials. For example, he filled identical bottles with different coloured liquids and placed them in a box to create colour fields. Pieces of white cardboard, all of the same size, but with different coloured backs and each with a cut-out "window" slightly smaller than the board before, were aligned so that the coloured back of each board slightly tinted the next white board in the row, creating changing colour variations depending on the light conditions.

Brunner was primarily interested in variable images and aesthetic structures which could be individually changed. He first realized this idea with objects created by assembling metre rules sprayed in one colour and mounted on a background of a different colour. The metre rule was anchored at a single point and the image could be changed and recreated by pushing or swivelling the individual joints of the metre rule against the background. A ten-part metre rule could thus provide a line broken in nine places which could also be positioned so that it

protruded beyond the edges of the background or base. In making the line a design element equal to the background plane, the latter lost its framework function and became part of the structure.

Edy Brunner took this concept one step further by dividing the metre rules into two sections of equal size and mounting each half on the surface so that it could be swivelled, then affixing a square aluminium plaque to each segment of the rule. This created more complex structures. The square format of the small aluminium plaques, in one colour or in several colours, reiterated the motif of the background or base and repeated it serially.

Literature:

M. Hölzel: Edy Brunner und Marc Kuhn in "Fourmière". In: Volksrecht, Winterthur, 23 November 1967 (Kulturspiegel)

fbr. (Fritz Billeter): Gezielte and weniger gezielte Experimente. In: Tages-Anzeiger, Zurich, 30 November 1967, p. 21

Circle Works

1967

Corrugated sheet metal, mobile
50 x 50 cm

Aluminium, anodized (metal and ochre), mobile
50 x 50 cm
Sticker on back: KREISE 1967 EDY BRUNNER

Aluminium, anodized (metal and black), mobile
50 x 50 cm

Inspired by Daniel Spoerri's 1959 "Edition MAT" (multiplication d'art transformable) Edy Brunner aimed to create a similar series of mobile multiples together with some young artist friends in Bern in 1967. They created a number of prototypes for discussion. They presented the works to Harald Szeemann who gave a statement on each piece and questioned the concept of an edition. In the end, the idea was abandoned.

Edy Brunner's prototype is a mobile "circle work" of corrugated metal. It consists of a flat box of finely corrugated sheet metal with a circular window at the front, through which the spectator can see six staggered circles of the same material. These circles are cut so that each one is smaller than the next. The last panel, which is not cut, forms the final plane of the object. All six circles are mobile and can be moved around, offering a wide variety of visual possibilities. The structure of the corrugated metal creates some interesting light effects reminiscent of Heinz Mack's kinetic light dynamos of the early 60s. Earlier variations of the object in different coloured anodized aluminium (metal/ochre, metal/black) did not achieve the same impact.

The visual possibilities of mobile concentric circles had already been examined in 1920 by Marcel Duchamp and realized in his roto-reliefs of the 30s and 50s before being systematically explored in the 50s and 60s by artists of the Zero Group. Few of these, however, offered the spectator as many possibilities of individual intervention as did the circle works by Edy Brunner.

Literature:
Edy Brunner. Marc Kuhn. (Exhibition catalogue). Zurich: Galerie La Fourmière, 1967

fbr. (Fritz Billeter): Gezielte und weniger gezielte Experimente. In: Tages-Anzeiger, Zurich, 30 November 1967, p. 21

GF: Der Uetiker Edy Brunner im Bülacher Sigristenkeller. In: Zürichsee-Zeitung, 27 March 1972

Gustav Ineichen (ed.): AMBAUEN, BRUNNER, DEL BONDIO, EISENEGGER, GASSER, GERBER. Rome: Istituto Svizzero di Roma, 1971/72

Roadblock Signs

1968

Multiple
(Sold in a plastic bag to be assembled by the owner)
Wood, red/white, mobile
72 x 88 cm
Edition of 50

Edy Brunner's later credo "I am a concrete artist" sheds some light on the intellectual origins of this multiple. As in the variable works by Karl Gerstner, these are primarily components for a concrete image to be assembled in any one of many different possible forms. The semiotic value of the signs has been translated into an autonomous visual factor by dividing a red and white roadblock sign into five pieces of equal size within a prescribed system (five components to be placed in any order inside a metal frame). Whereas the prototype was created using a conventional roadblock sign, the multiples were made out of specially manufactured components. The basis for this object is once again the found object or prefabricated component. By clearly indicating the origin of the multiple in the title, the artist draws attention to the unexpected aesthetic qualities of everyday items.

Literature:

BRUNNER GUTMANN BEI: GALERIE BRECHBÜHL GRENCHEN. (Exhibition catalogue). Grenchen: Galerie Brechbühl, 1968

Socket Cubes

1968

35 black and white plastic sockets on a wooden frame linked
by black and white cables with plugs
44 x 44 x 9.5 cm
Verso: 1968 EDY BRUNNER

30 black and white plastic sockets on cubic wood relief, linked
by black and white cables with plugs
46 x 49 x 18 cm
Verso: 1968 EDY BRUNNER

18 black and white plastic sockets on cubic wood relief, linked
by black and white cables with plugs
Multiple
37 x 38 x 11.5 cm
Edition of 5
Sticker on back: MULTIPLE-STECKER 1968 1/5 BRUNNER / EDY
BRUNNER

Edy Brunner showed his first individually variable aesthetic
structures in November/December 1967 at his exhibition at the
Galerie La Fourmière, Zurich. Apart from his metre rule works
and circle works, he had created objects made of rows of
plastic sockets to be linked at will by cables with plugs. He continued to vary and modify this design principle several times in
1967/68. In this way, he created a group of works marking a
new phase in Edy Brunner's artistic development.

Strongly influenced by his work as a retoucher and graphic
artist, Edy Brunner experimented primarily with paper and cardboard in his early works during the period 1964-66 and soon
found he had exhausted the technical possibilities of these
media. It was during his practical training as an industrial
designer 1966/67 with Hans Kronenberg in Lucerne that he
first gained some experience in handling such materials as
metal and wood. This was to have an influence on his art. By
the time he made his metre rule works, Brunner was using
anodized aluminium plaques. His circle works were made entirely of metal. He went even further with his socket works.
Here, he used prefabricated components, wrenched out of
their familiar functional setting and placed them in a new
aesthetic context. Positioning them serially in a row further
alienated these objects in a remarkable way.

Two works based on this principle were exhibited in 1967.
These are a relief of 25 white 5-by-5 sockets assembled in a
square and linked by several black cables and plugs (no longer
extant) and a stele of 10 black sockets mounted on top of each
other linked by white cables and plugs (no longer extant).
Later, he created objects of increasing difference and spatial
handling. A cubic object made of 19 cubes whose sides were
covered by 9 (3 x 3) black or white sockets linked with a
number of white and black cables with plugs of the same
colour is the most spatially intensive of these series. For this
work, Edy Brunner was awarded a grant by the Kiefer-Hablitzel-
Foundation in 1968.

Literature:

BRUNNER GUTMANN BEI GALERIE BRECHBÜHL GRENCHEN. (Exhibition catalogue).
Grenchen: Galerie Brechbühl, 1968

LG: Aufforderung zum (ersten) Spiel. Zwei interessante Gestalter stellen in der Galerie
Brechbühl aus. In: Grenchner Tagblatt, Grenchen, 10 May 1968, p. 47

EF: Junge Kunst auf alten und neuen Wegen. Stipendienausstellung 1968 der Kiefer-Hablitzel-
Stiftung. In: Luzerner Neueste Nachrichten, 7 October 1968, p. 6

Willy Rotzler: Renaissance der Objekt-Kunst nach 1945. In: du, Zurich, September 1969,
p. 675

Moderne Kunst in der IBM Schweiz: In IBM MOSAIC, Zurich, 10. Jg., 1/March 1971,
p. 10 (variation)

Gustav Ineichen (ed.): AMBAUEN, BRUNNER, DEL BONDIO, EISENEGGER, GASSER, GERBER.
Rome: Istituto Svizzero di Roma, 1971/72

Willy Rotzler: OBJEKT-KUNST. Von Duchamp bis Kienholz. Cologne: Verlag DuMont
Schauber, 1972, p. 186

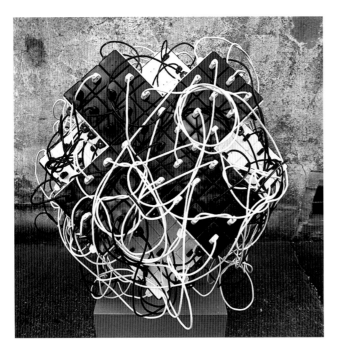

Wherever the artist combines large quantities of identical, mass manufactured products to create an art work, the individual item possesses hardly any quality as a distinctive object in its own right. It is the raw material of design, and only through its repeated or even mass projection can it be recognised as an object once more. Above all, the assembly of such ready-mades takes on the character of an object itself. This is certainly true of the reliefs and cubic objects created by the young Swiss artist Edy Brunner using electrical components such as plugs and cables. They appear as meaningless, useless items whose material and formal characteristics nevertheless clearly express the concept of communication, modification and interruption of all connections.

Willy Rotzler
Renaissance der Objekt-Kunst nach 1945 (Renaissance of Object Art after 1945) published in "du" magazine, Zürich, September 1969, p. 675)

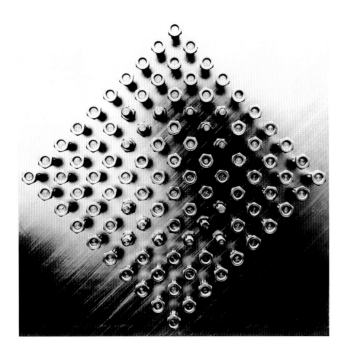

1968

100 iron bolts and nuts affixed to a metal plate
Iron, bromatized
89 x 89 cm (no longer extant)

Prefabricated or found materials continued to inspire Edy Brunner to create new works. He was not interested in the concept of the art work as a unique and unrepeatable artefact. In what Walter Benjam termed the "age of technical reproducibility", the art work must necessarily be redefined. Since the birth of the ready-made, a new dimension had been opened up in the way art was perceived. Reproducibility now became an inherent factor in an entire genre of artistic solutions.

The intellectual game with ready-mades and ready-mades aidés continued to attract Edy Brunner, inspiring him to find artistic solutions that would reflect our modern times and technical fetishism. Bolts and nuts, hardly artistic objects when regarded on their own, gain an entirely new appeal when stringently positioned in rows, robbed of their original function and presented as elements of an aesthetic system. What is more, they make us aware of the beauty of the individual item. In this way, the artist opens our eyes to everyday objects whose form is determined entirely by their practical purpose and which are interesting in their own way.

For this object (as well as for the socket cubes) Edy Brunner received a grant from the Kiefer-Hablitzel Foundation in 1968.

The bolts were affixed to a metal plate with Araldite adhesive and after a while they began to come loose again. He continued to experiment with the bolts that had fallen off and it was this that developed into the triple bolt multiple. He created a further bolt relief using coloured anodized nuts.

Literature:

BRUNNER GUTMANN BEI GALERIE BRECHBÜHL GRENCHEN. (Exhibition catalogue). Grenchen: Galerie Brechbühl, 1968

Triple Bolt

1968

Multiple, adjustable, iron, bromatized, 8.5 x 8 x 8 cm
Stamped on the outside of one nut: EDY BRUNNER / (number)
Edition of 50

This object consists of three adjacent nuts (size M 24) with bolts reduced to the threaded main body alone. Each of the bolts can be adjusted at will within the nut. The astonishing effect of playing with this possibility is that whatever the position of the bolt and the slant of the object, the overall impression is completely different – yet it still seems stable. In each position, the bolts are parallel and their upper points create a surface which is also parallel to the base. Over and above the visual appeal of this work, it has enormous textural appeal. It seems to have a kind of magic hold on our attention. As we grasp it, move it around, play with it, the way we see nuts and bolts is changed.

Literature:

Gustav Ineichen (ed.): AMBAUEN, BRUNNER, DEL BONDIO, EISENEGGER, GRASSER, GERBER.
Rome: Istituto Svizzero di Roma, 1971/72

Playgirls

1968

18 Shutter clips, iron, bromatized, mounted on red anodized aluminium plate, mobile
49.5 x 45 cm
Verso: PLAYGIRLS 1968 / EDY BRUNNER

1969

5 Shutter clips, iron, bromatized, mounted together on deep-drawn black Plexiglas plate
Multiple
37.5 x 37.5 cm
Edition of 20

The explicitly sexual connotation of the title contrasts sharply with the innocent-looking figures of demurely hatted girls. Decorative clips used to hold louvred shutters open become fetishes highlighting the petty bourgeois ideal of home comforts; mounted in a regular grid-like pattern on a square aluminium plate in anodized red and provocatively inviting us to play, and with a highly ambiguous title, they become the object of conceptual humour. Five shutter-holders in a row on a deep-drawn black plexiglass slab was later made into a multiple by Brunner.

Here, for the first time, we encounter an intellectual mechanism that is to become a basic feature of many later works by this artist: the confusion aroused by a contradiction in terms, either by visualizing concepts which cannot be visualized or by inventing an absurd title for the work. Marcel Duchamp is clearly a point of reference here. There is both intellectual and sensual appeal in the way these "playgirls" have been located somewhere between erotic fantasy, alienation of the individual object and playful action.

Literature:

GF: Der Uetiker Edy Brunner im Bülacher Sigristenkeller. In: Zürichsee-Zeitung, 27 March 1972, p. 6

rs: Im Bülacher Sigristenkeller: "Brunner kommt". In: Tages-Anzeiger, 30 March 1972, p. 57

Plastic Clothes

1969

Multiple
Plastic, deep-drawn, wire coat-hanger
80 x 43 x 2 cm
Size of edition unknown

In 1968, for a Zurich boutique, Edy Brunner developed a package for clothes in the form of a deep-drawn plastic jacket. He produced one prototype model, but it did not go into serial production. A Dow Chemical Europe S.A. advertising campaign for dry cleaning, for which he designed the plastic jacket with a wire coat-hanger (like those used by dry cleaning companies) was not realized. Nevertheless, the object met with so much acclaim that he had it produced as a multiple in a relatively large quantity.

This was Brunner's "deep-draw phase", as he calls it himself. During this period, he explored the technology of deep-drawing as a relatively economical means of producing objects. The influence of Pop Art is evident in this exaggerated presentation of everyday objects, such as plastic jackets, hands holding a writing block, the 23,688 little TV frames of his conceptual tableau "Apollo 11", his "Philodendron for everyone"

made of serially produced leaves, stems and pots to be assembled at will, or the relief of a dangling lightbulb as the base of the poster for a performance of Franz Hohler's *"Nachtübung"* at the Theater am Hechtplatz in Zurich.

Literature:

Gustav Ineichen (ed.): AMBAUEN, BRUNNER, DEL BONDIO, EISENEGGER, GASSER, GERBER. Rome: Istituto Svizzero di Roma, 1971/72

rs: Im Bülacher Sigristenkeller: "Brunner kommt". In: Tages-Anzeiger, 30 March 1972, p. 57

Leonardo Bezzola: "BRUNNER KAM". In: werk, Zurich, 6/1972, p. 339

"St Gotthard Tunnel" Documentation

1969

Serial tableau of 1144 small-format black and white photos
mounted in individual frames
1 tableau
100 x 313 cm
Inscription on back: St Gotthard Tunnel, 1969, 1,144 photographs taken at one second intervals
Staatsgalerie Stuttgart (acquired from the collection of Dr Rolf H. Krauss, Stuttgart)

As for many other young Swiss artists of his generation, the exhibition *"Wenn Attitüden Form werden"* organised by Harald Szeemann from 22.3. to 27.4.1969 at the Kunsthalle Bern was a key event that was to have a profound influence on his art. The exhibition presented the latest international developments in contemporary conceptual art. *"Live in Your Head"* was the theme of the show. Its common denominator was the attempt to formulate aspects of a new view of reality: ... *apparent opposition to form; a high degree of personal and emotional commitment; declaring as art things that were previously not identified as art; shifting the emphasis of interest from the result to the procedure; the use of poor materials; the interaction of work and material ...* (Harald Szeeman in the catalogue of the 1969 Bern exhibition.)

The process itself as an important element of the art work was to become the basis of Edy Brunner's search for appropriate forms of expression. He achieved the documentation and presentation of an event with the aid of a technical medium by adopting the principle of recording a process on film in real time, breaking it down into individual phases and presenting these simultaneously so that the time factor was filtered out of the end result. His first project of this kind involved documenting a 19-minute train ride through the St Gotthard Tunnel.

A 36 mm film camera with single-frame exposure installed in the driver's cab of a locomotive shot one frame per second on the way through the tunnel. The film was then enlarged and printed on photographic paper. Each image was individually framed and mounted on a panel in a horizontal sequence of 22 strips, whereby the space-time process can be perceived simultaneously on an area of 2,800 cm.

By 1969, the photographic exploration of time and space was already well advanced. Dennis Oppenheim and many others were working with landscape. That same year, Jan Dibbets created his "Flood Tide", a 10-part documentation of the incoming tide shot over a period of two hours, with the individual images mounted together. Nowhere, however, is the principle of succession, one of the two art forms that photography has discovered for itself, so lucidly presented as

in this work by Edy Brunner. (Rolf H. Krauss in "Kunst mit Photographie", op.cit.)

For this "incunable of succession" as it has been described by Stefan Frey and Marc Joachim Wasmer in "Mit erweitertem Auge" (op.cit., p. 107) the artist was awarded a federal art grant in 1971.

Literature:

The Swiss Avant Garde. (Exhibition catalogue). New York: New York Cultural Center, 1971, p. 87, cat. no. 17

4a BIENNALE DI BOLZANO. (Exhibition catalogue). Bolzano, 1971, p. 152 f.

Walter Aue: P.C.A. Prozesse, Concepte & Actionen. Cologne: Verlag DuMont Schauberg, 1971

Gustav Ineichen (ed.): AMBAUEN. BRUNNER. DEL BONDIO. EISENEGGER. GASSER. GERBER. Rome: Istituto Svizzero di Roma, 1971/72

Rolf H. Krauss / Manfred Schmalriede / Michael Schwarz. Kunst mit Photographie. Die Sammlung Dr. Rolf H. Krauss. (Exhibition catalogue). Berlin: Verlag Fröhlich & Kaufmann, 1983, cat. no. 42, p. 106 f., p. 323

Stefan Frey (ed.): Mit erweitertem Auge. Berner Künstler und die Fotografie. (Exhibition catalogue). Bern: Bernische Stiftung für Fotografie, Film und Video (FFV)/Bentelli Verlag, 1986, p. 106 f.

Urs Stahel / Martin Heller. Fotografie in der Schweiz. Wichtige Bilder. (Exhibition catalogue). Zurich: Der Alltag / Museum für Gestaltung, 1990, p. 178

Page 25:
"St Gotthard Tunnel" tableau
(details below)

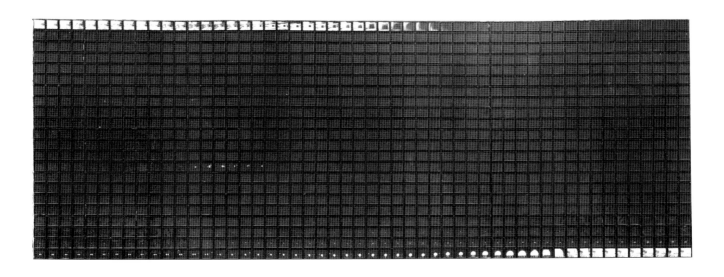

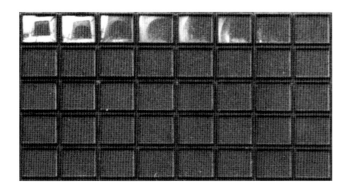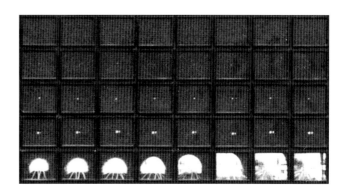

"Apollo 11" Documentation

1969

Serial tableau of 23,688 small format colour photos
mounted in individual frames
11 tableaux
170 x 960 cm

"Apollo 11", the first manned landing on the moon, captured the imagination of all who saw it on television or heard about it on the radio. Edy Brunner wanted to create a work that would reflect something of the overwhelming effect this event had on people. An individual artistic commentary did not seem appropriate to him. The work should have a supra-individual character. To this end, he installed a film camera rigged with individual frame switch in front of a colour TV, shooting a frame each second so that the entire live transmission, from the preparation for lift-off to the triumphant return of the astronauts and their welcome by the US President, was documented.

The films were printed onto photographic paper using a CIBA-chrome process. The artist mounted each single image in a specially created plastic frame resembling a TV screen and placed these tiny TV screens in rows, in a vertical sequence, on 11 panels. He then joined these panels to create a single large tableau almost 10 m in length. The 23,688 small colour TV screens thus created a kind of frozen fast-motion image of the event as seen by millions of TV spectators throughout the world. In contrast to the St. Gotthard documentation, this is not the direct implementation of a process. Although it is also recorded in real time, the event here has already been filtered by the TV transmission symbolized by the TV screen frames. There can be no doubt that, once again, the artist has created a work of outstanding originality. The impressive format breaks with convention and pays homage to the enterprise which, until then, had been beyond most people's wildest dreams ("a small step for a man, but a great step for mankind").

The work triggered heated debates amongst the judges responsible for the allocation of federal art grants in 1970: was this actually art, or was it applied art (i.e. a purely photographic work)? In the end, the conceptual character of the work was recognized as its predominant feature, with photography serving merely as the vehicle. The (then unfinished) tableau was declared a work of art and Edy Brunner became the first to be awarded this federal fine arts grant for a photographically produced image.

When Herbert Distel asked Edy Brunner to provide a miniature work for his "Museum of Drawers", the artist submitted a single TV frame from the Apollo tableau showing a TV still of the three happily landed astronauts with the title "Apollo 11, 1:24.000".

Literature:

p.d. Ein Kunststipendium für 24,000 Farbfotos. In: Zürichsee-Zeitung 10 March 1970, p.21

"Apollo 11" Dokumentationsbild mit dem Eidgenössischen Kunstipendium ausgezeichnet. In: Meilener Anzeiger, 13 March 1970

P.H. (Hans Held): "Dokumentationsbild Apollo 11". In: Ringiers Unterhaltungs-Blätter, Zofingen, 18 April 1970, p. 50

J.H.M.: Das Mondlandeunternehmen Apollo 11 in 24.000 Farbfotos. In: Tages-Anzeiger, Zurich, 14 July 1970

4a BIENNALE DI BOLZANO. (Exhibition catalogue). Bolzano, 1971, p. 152 f.

Walter Aue: P.C.A. Projecte. Concepte & Actionen. Cologne: Verlag DuMont Schauberg, 1971

Gustav Ineichen (ed.): AMBAUEN, BRUNNER, DEL BONDIO, EISENEGGER, GASSER, GERBER. Rome: Istituto Svizzero di Roma, 1971/72

Herbert Distel: Das Schubladenmuseum. La musée en tiroirs. The Museum of Drawers. (Exhibition catalogue). Zurich: Kunsthaus, 1978, p. 23, 39

Page 26:
Edy Brunner with the tableaux

Page 27:
individual tableau

Pages 28 – 31:
details

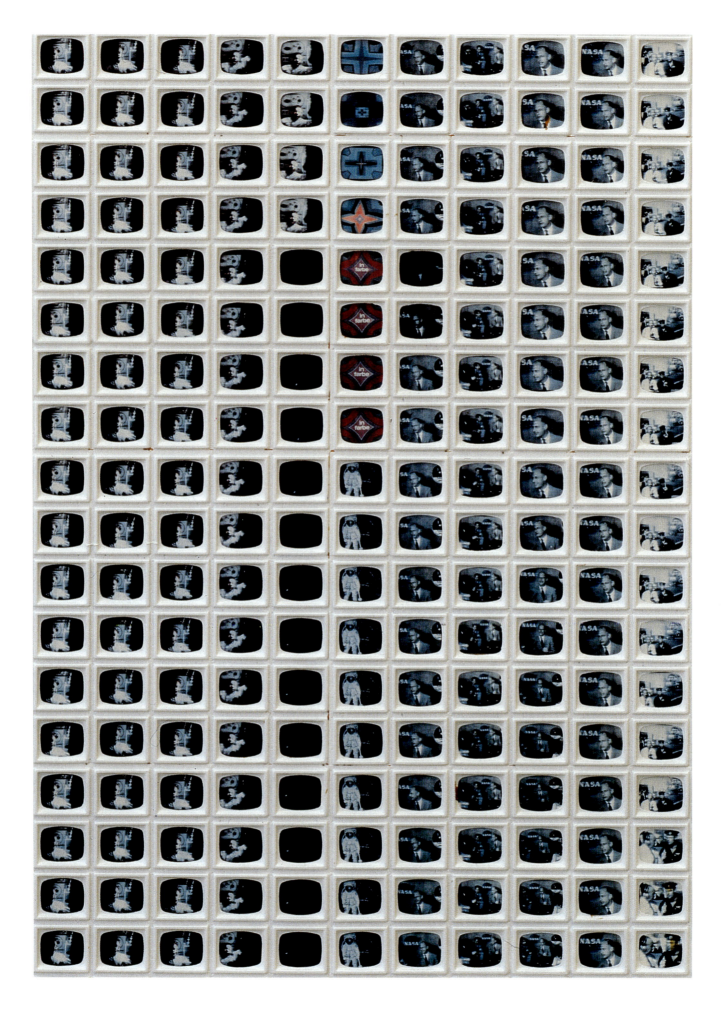

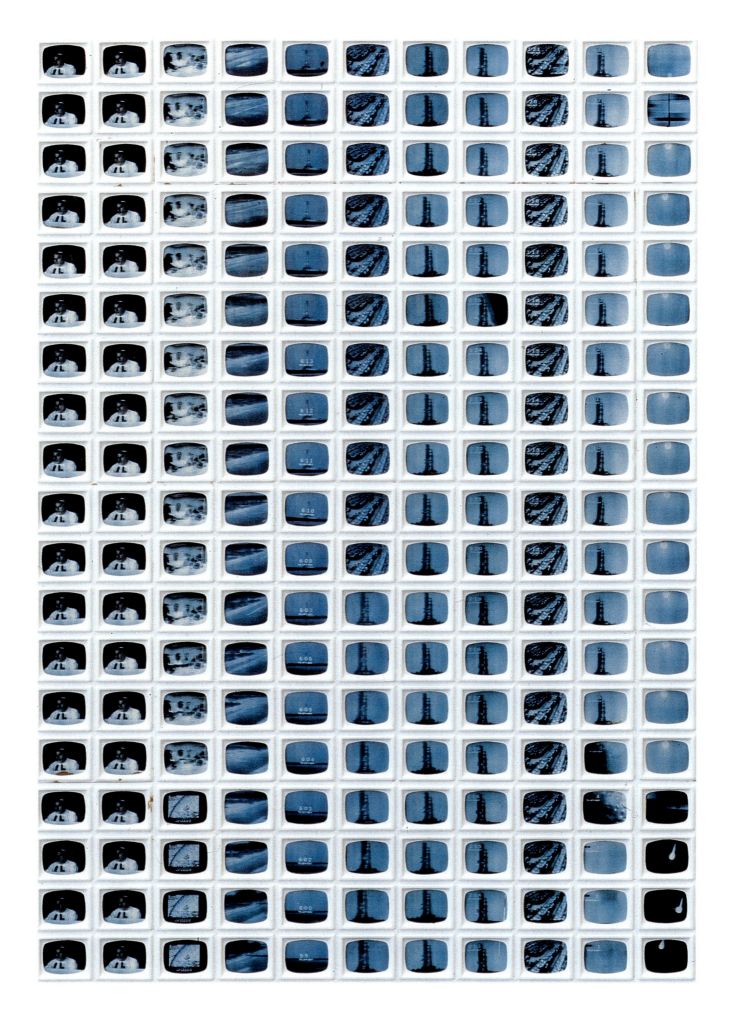

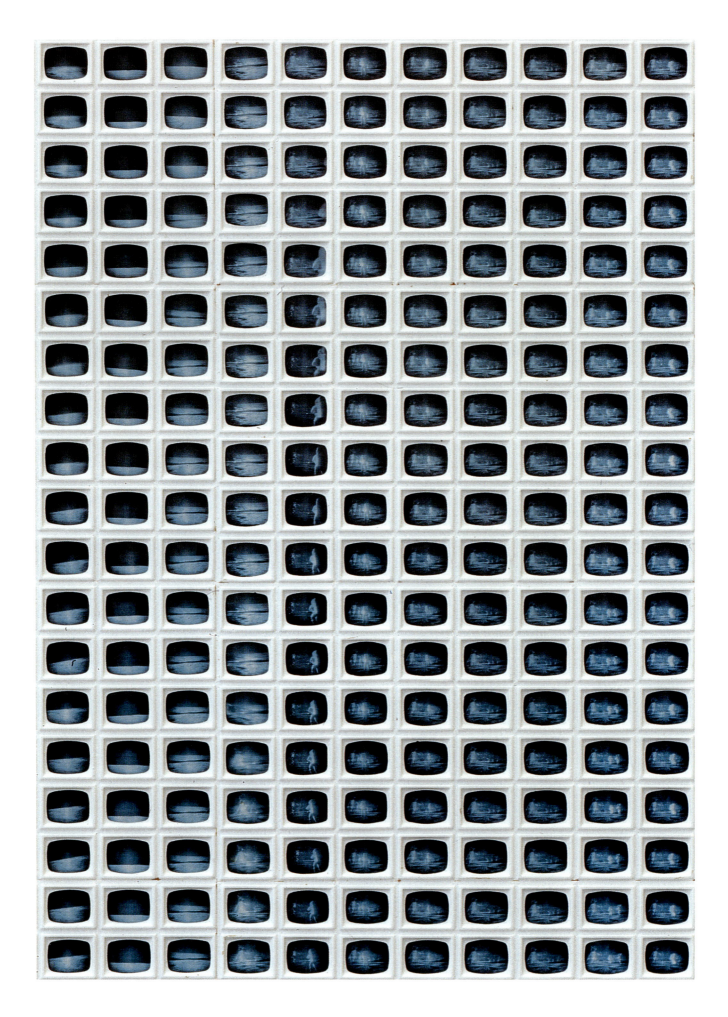

"Trans Atlantic" Documentation

1970/86

Contribution to the "Canaries" project

Serial tableau consisting of 2,240 colour photos (35 mm),
mounted in individual frames
1 tableau
120 x 235 cm

Following the concept of Swiss artist Herbert Distel, a polyester egg (L 3 m, Ø 2 m) was produced in 1970 and placed in the Atlantic Ocean at the Canary Islands, where it was carried by the Canary Current, the Equatorial Current, the Antilla Current and the Florida Current, driven by the Passat winds, crossing the ocean and landing on the eastern seaboard of Central American after a voyage of some three months. This event was described by Herbert Distel as the "first solo Atlantic crossing by an art work". As in the journey through the St. Gotthard tunnel, Edy Brunner installed a film camera in the egg, rigged to take a single frame shot every 20 minutes and thus document the journey in serial form. The film created in this way was intended as a fast-motion document and as the basis for a serial tableau. For his part in this project, together with the tableaux "St. Gotthard-Tunnel" and "Self-Portrait", the artist was awarded a federal art grant in 1971.

About six months after its release, the egg was found smashed on the rocks of the Venezuelan coast. A year later, the Swiss Embassy in Venezuela sent Edy Brunner the film, which had been badly damaged by seawater. It also turned out that the camera was faulty and had run faster than planned. Nevertheless, he restored the film, which documents the first five nights and days of the journey. The tableau, however, was not mounted until 1986 when it was shown in the exhibition "Mit erweitertem Auge – Berner Künstler und die Fotografie" (at the Kunstmuseum in Bern 4 September – 26 October 1986).

Literature:

M. Bruell/J.H. Bruell: Ein Ei geht auf Reisen. In: Neue Zürcher Zeitung, 17 May 1970

Jürg H. Meyer: Ein Ei auf Herrn Kolumbus' Spuren. In: Tages-Anzeiger, Zurich, 21 May 1970

The Swiss Avant Garde. (Exhibition catalogue). New York: New York Cultural Center, 1971, p. 86

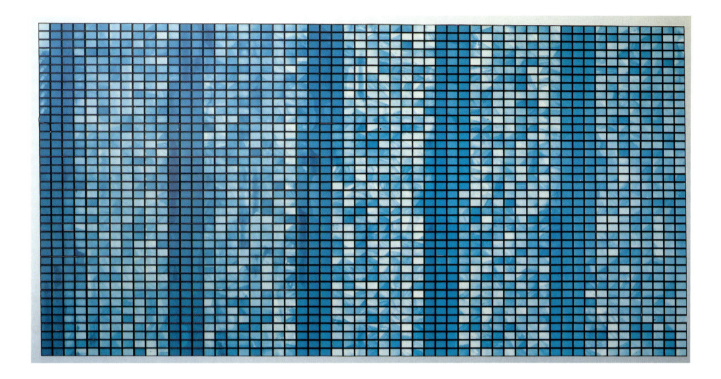

Self-Portrait

1970

Serial tableau of 264 black and white photos (35 mm),
mounted in individual frames
49.5 x 129.5 cm/59 x 139 cm

It was the simultaneity of processes on a single plane in his successive and documentary images that inspired Edy Brunner to experiment with a three-dimensional object. In the history of European art, this is certainly nothing new. For a long time, central perspective seemed to be the best way of representing three-dimensionality on a surface. In the early 20th century, the Cubists addressed this issue by painterly means, showing all views of the object represented simultaneously.

Edy Brunner sought a method which would exclude subjective influences in the process of documentation and which therefore has a higher degree of objectivity than the paintings of the Cubists. Drawing upon his experience in the field of photography, he had his own head photographed all round, systematically and field by field using a 24 x 36 camera. The result is a topographically precise image of his own head as a three-dimensional object. The grid created by the individual frames corresponds to a system of coordinates. The only intervention by the artist is his definition of the grid.

Later variations on this principle, such as the Polaroid portrayals of entire bodies by English artist David Hockney in the 70s, did not achieve the conceptual stringency of Edy Brunner's self-portrait.

Literature:

The Swiss Avant Garde. (Exhibition catalogue). New York: New York Cultural Center, 1971, p. 87, cat.no. 18

Walter Aue: P.C.A. Projecte, Concepte & Actionen. Cologne: Verlag DuMont Schauberg, 1971

Gustav Ineichen (ed.): AMBAUEN, BRUNNER, DEL BONDIO, EISENEGGER, GASSER, GERBER. Rome: Istituto Svizzero di Roma, 1971/72

Leonardo Bezzola: "BRUNNER KAM". In: werk, Zurich, 6/1972, p. 338

Stefan Frey (ed.): Mit erweitertem Auge. Berner Künstler und die Fotografie. (Exhibition catalogue). Bern: Bernische Stiftung für Fotografie, Film und Video (FFV)/Benteli Verlag, 1986, p. 105

Urs Stahel/Martin Heller: Fotografie in der Schweiz. Wichtige Bilder. (Exhibition catalogue). Zurich: Der Alltag/Museum für Gestaltung, 1990, p. 170, 190

"Swiss Parliament" documentary images

1972

Federal Councillors
Serial tableau (portrait accumulation)
7 black and white photos, each mounted inside a white plastic
cross on a red background
(no longer extant)

Members of Parliament
Serial tableau (portrait accumulation)
244 black and white photos, each mounted in a white plastic
cross on a red background
125 x 240 cm (no longer extant)

While he was living in Rome, Edy Brunner had the idea of using
his documentary images to portray social contexts. He was fascinated by the idea of presenting something as complex and
intangible as a country's parliament in an objective form while
creating room for the interpretation of a difficult and inter-
related fabric. For the Swiss Parliament, the cross seemed an
appropriate symbol. He framed a photo of each Swiss parlia-
mentarian of the year 1972 in a white plastic cross. By accumu-
lating individual elements of equal size in this way, the artist
also evokes the basic tenet of modern democracy: the equality
of all citizens. Like the people they portray, the photos can be
replaced. In this way, the tableau can be constantly updated.
The images are dovetailed in a way that suggests they are in-
extricably interwoven, whereby Brunner makes no distinction
between "interwoven" and "embroiled". Originally, there
were plans for an accompanying brochure documenting the
involvement of the individual parliamentarians in politics and
industry, but this was not published.

Literature:

Gustav Ineichen (ed.): AMBAUEN, BRUNNER, DEL BONDIO, EISENEGGER, GASSER, GERBER.
Rome: Istituto Svizzero di Roma, 1971/72

GF: Der Uetiker Edy Brunner im Bülacher Sigristenkeller. In: Zürichsee-Zeitung, 27 March
1972, p. 6

rs.: Im Bülacher Sigristenkeller: "Brunner kommt". In: Tages-Anzeiger, Zurich, 30 March
1972, p. 57

Leonardo Bezzola: "BRUNNER KAM". In: werk, Zurich, 6/1972, p. 339

z.: Wenn man sich Rosen schenkt – in Bern. In: Der Bund, Bern, 13 October 1972, p. 43

pjb.: Berner Galerie: Press-Art und Edi Brunner. In: Berner Tagblatt, 23 October 1972, p. 9

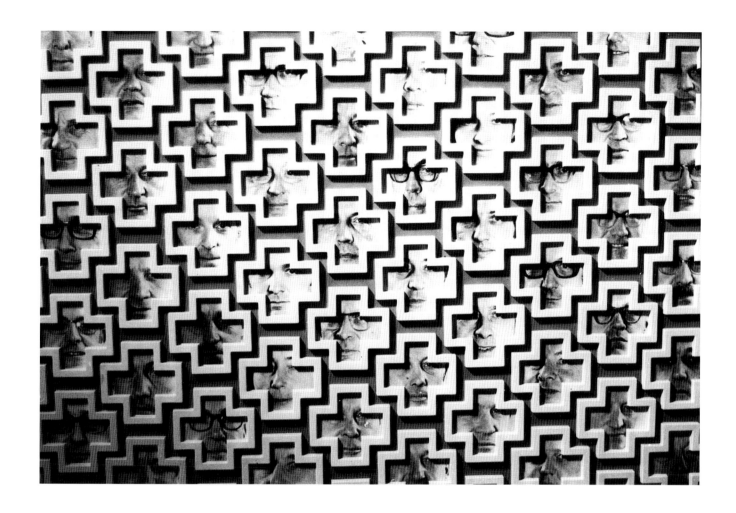

Three roses for your friends, their friends and their friends

1972

Multiple
3 artificial roses (one colour: yellow, red or pink) in a plastic
bag, with a booklet attached in German, French, English
and Italian
63.5 x 34 x 7 cm
Edition of 20

Presents can often pose a problem. What should you offer your
host? The act of giving is an obligatory gesture of politeness;
we all know what Edy Brunner has described as "that famous
box of chocolates, never opened and invariably passed on".
The artist was so amused by this idea of "circulating gifts" that
he made this the point of departure for a multiple aimed at
serving precisely that purpose. Three artificial roses in specially
made plastic bags, each with a little leaflet in which the person
giving the rose or passing it on is registered until the circle
finally closes and the original owner receives the gift again and
can follow its path by referring to the leaflet.

The text in four languages by Peter Held reads: *A present of
three roses creates pleasure and friends. A present of three
roses that last for ever creates more pleasure and more friends.
A tip from the gardener: Roses belong to nature's most delicate
flowers. By opening this bag these roses may be damaged.
Handled carefully, they will last for ever.* What is more, some
things are better said with flowers. For lovers that usually
means roses. In these fast-living times of ours, love affairs tend
to change with increasing frequency. This leads, of course, to
an inevitable increase in the consumption of roses. Brunner's
object alleviates the situation. It is an object for all seasons: a
gift, a keepsake, something to pass on or to return.

This multiple has a conceptual wit that functions on several
different levels: the circulating gift as an expression of increasingly superficial interpersonal relationships, the gesture of
politeness as a ritual devoid of meaning. The artist has allocated an unexpected communicative function to this gift for
the host. After all, there is a certain intimacy in receiving the
same gift again (a kind of do-as-you-would-be-done-by effect).
What is more, it is a distinctly tongue-in-cheek commentary on
today's throwaway relationships, perhaps with a view to our
own experience. The fact that he uses artificial flowers that can
never wilt – just as one wishes that love itself will never fade,
may be a reference to self-delusion and false sentiment. In any
case, this little bouquet is the most intelligent imaginable form
of camouflage in the field of loving gifts.

Literature:
z.: Wenn man sich Rosen schenkt – in Bern. In: Der Bund, Bern, 13 October 1972, p. 437

1972

Multiple
Artificial rose on a green plastic base, in a transparent plastic
cover (to be arranged in any quantity)
60 x 25 x 25 cm

flowers in it. In the end, he abandoned the idea of using any
natural flowers, thereby heightening the criticism expressed in
this work

Literature:

z.: Wenn man sich Rosen schenkt - in Bern. In: Der Bund, Bern, 13 October 1972, p. 43

The artificial flower is a never-fading substitute for nature; that,
at least, is the idea behind it. Brunner takes this idea one step
further with the glaring artificiality of his presentation and by
isolating each individual rose in a plastic cover. Finally, the addition of these individual identical objects heightens the concept
ad absurdum: the constant availability of this indestructible
surrogate that can survive the worst possible environmental
damage. The artist addresses one of the existential problems of
our day with the razor-edge of his finely tempered wit. He does
not formulate a direct protest against air pollution. Instead, he
makes a comment on a fundamental attitude towards nature.

Edy Brunner developed the idea for this multiple while he
was living in Rome in 1971/72, where he began to address the
social problems of urban planning and ecology that were to
occupy him for many years. He originally planned filling the
blossom of a large artificial rose with earth and growing new

Heuried Housing Project, Zürich-Wiedikon

1972–76

Environmental design
In collaboration with Karl Schneider

In a statement written in Rome in spring 1972, Edy Brunner wrote: *I want to be involved in housing projects, in designing an environment for living, in planning such environments for people of all ages. I do not want to bring my art into the world in the form of individual works. I want to make it accessible to as many people as possible within the context of a wider living environment. In this respect, I regard art as a contribution to life in the community. (Quoted in: Gustav Ineichen (ed.): AMABUEN. BRUNNER. DEL BONDIO. EISENEGGER. GASSER. GERBER. op.cit.)*

Edy Brunner pursued this concept for the first time in his environmental designs for the Heuried housing project. Built in the 1920s, the housing project was condemned in 1966 and replaced in the years that followed by a redevelopment scheme under the direction of architects Peter Leemann and Claude Paillard. Edy Brunner was invited to submit ideas for the environmental design at the project planning phase, and, together with the designer Karl Schneider, he was thus able to introduce his ideas into the project at a very early stage.

The aim was to create a distinctive atmosphere with excellent communication facilities so that the residents could enjoy a good social climate and identify with their immediate environment, something rarely achieved in new housing projects and frequently a fundamental problem of low-income housing.

Collaborating with the project architects at such an early stage of development made it possible to merge certain budgetary aspects, permitting a high degree of efficiency, while allowing all the parties involved to develop complex solutions so that it was not just a question of superimposing "art" on a completed project (as the client's social alibi) but of integrating it fully into the overall planning of the project as a whole, in an exemplary way. The enthusiastic reactions in the press and specialized literature bear witness to the success of this approach. The project was also presented at the Venice Biennale in 1976.

The most eye-catching feature is the portrayal of different profiles on the house facades, lending the architecture a degree of individuality and transporting democratic ideas by presenting the "man on the street". The overall atmosphere was intended to foster a sense of community within the individual housing units and in the project as a whole. The artists designed the inner courtyard as a large, landscaped plaza, covered partly with gravel and partly with concrete cobbles, with individual objects such as a "hill of ruins" featuring old architectural elements, a "spring hill" with a fountain, a "slide hill", a "ship", whose funnels wittily camouflage the ventilation of the air-raid shelters below, etc.. All these objects can be used by all the residents; there are no sections intended specifically for children or senior citizens, for example.

Trees planted in a triangular grid structure (5 x 5 x 5 m) screen off the court and living areas, giving a sense of shelter.

Another way of actively involving individuals in the design of their own environment is Brunner's idea of getting the residents to paint their own letterboxes. The paints were provided and the residents participated enthusiastically and competitively, adding to the sense of communication between them and allowing them to identify more fully with their environment. The exceptionally well-kept appearance of the housing project as a whole, almost 20 years on, bears eloquent witness to this.

Literature:

Siedlung mit Gesicht. In: Züri Leu, Zürich, 18 June 1976, p. 19

G.R.: Die Wohnsiedlung Heuried und Utohof in Wiedikon. In: Neue Zürcher Zeitung, Zürich, 22 June 1976

Schweiz. Suisse, Svizzera. 37. Biennale von Venedig 1976. (Exhibition catalogue). Zürich: Eidgenössisches Amt für kulturelle Angelegenheiten, 1976

La Biennale di Venezia 1976. Environment, Participation, Cultural Structures. General Catalogue. First Volume. (Exhibition catalogue). Venice: Edizioni "LA BIENNALE DI VENEZIA", 1976, p. 144 ff

Wohnüberbauung Heuried in Zürich-Wiedikon. In: werk/oeuvre, St. Gallen, 12/1976, p. 828 ff.

Jean-Luc Daval (ed.): ART ACTUEL, SKIRA ANNUEL No. 3. Genève: Editions Skira et Cosmopress, 1977, p. 102

Wohnsiedlungen Heuried und Utohof Zürich-Wiedikon. Zürich: Stadt Zürich, September 1978

Breath of life. In: International Herald Tribune, London, 4 April 1979, p. 4

Everyday Apparel

1976/77

Mural for Zürich-Kloten Airport Railway Station

For the competition to decorate the platform walls of the newly built underground railway station at Zürich-Kloten Airport, Edy Brunner came up with a concept based on the idea that travellers arriving at and departing from the airport are constantly confronted with technical facilities and procedures which constitute a certain stress factor. In order to offset this, he sought a design solution that would appeal directly to the individual's love of looking and exploring, enhancing the experience of using the railway station and thus heightening the overall positive feeling. In this extremely public place, Brunner had no intention of simply developing visual art in the usual sense. He sought an idea beyond the norm, more original and likely to attract more attention to the design.

Brunner's intention was to capture the *zeitgeist* of the period in which the railway station was built so that the mural, apart from its artistic quality, would also take on a documentary character. As in earlier works, he used found objects as his point of departure and as his media for the work. His concept envisaged scattering clothes and everyday objects belonging to all kinds of people whose lives were related in some way to the airport and the railway station, and pressing these objects between plates of glass, vacuum-packed in a standard format and mounted on the wall. The objects included, for example, the uniforms of all the airlines using the airport, airport and railway station staff and security personnel, typical garments of a brass band and their pressed musical instruments, items of clothing belonging to famous people who had visited Zürich that year.

The items of clothing and other objects were to be spread over a large wall and then cut to fit into 1 x 1 metre glass components to be pressed between two glass plates and vacuum-packed in a steel frame for mounting. In this way, the glass components could easily be affixed to the station walls. Seen from three different distances and angles, the overall effect was very different. Seen from a distance, the wall appears to be covered in otherwise unidentifiable shapes and colours. Seen from the platform, the spectator observes sections and recognises the individual objects. What is perceived at a distance as an abstract overall structure is transformed by closer scrutiny into familiar objects from the immediate environment. In this way, the spectator's gaze is drawn to details and an interest in the individual objects is aroused. Through the windows of the trains, the design looks completely different yet again, as it is perceived at close quarters, framed by the coincidental section of the window. Travelling past slowly, the entire mural can be considered in its full length.

It is only through the movement of the traveller that the mural can be perceived from a variety of angles and distances and it is only through this process that it can be appreciated in its full conceptual and formal scope. By wrenching everyday objects out of their familiar context and presenting them in a different form – an important technique in Brunner's artistic oeuvre – they are revalued within an aesthetic system that stimulates a new approach to our own ways of seeing and thinking.

For the competition presentation, Brunner created a model on a scale of 1:1 and provisionally installed it on one wall of a platform at the railway station.

Model on a scale of 1:1, glass, steel, clothing

"Chempe"

1978–80

Environmental design with fountain
VITA life-insurance company grounds, Zürich-Wieding

On inviting designs for the corporate plaza in front of their building on Austrasse in Zürich-Wieding, the VITA insurance did not specify any thematic requirements. The only condition was that the artist should include water and use the boulders found during the excavation of the foundations. These "Chempe" (an old Bernese dialect word for stone) were to be the conceptual starting point for Edy Brunner's sculpture which was chosen as the winning design amongst the 34 submitted projects.

Edy Brunner's conceptual wit and his playful approach to questions of art and design are particularly in evidence here. As though by chance, he has scattered the huge boulders across this otherwise unremarkable area. It is as though they had been cast down from the heavens, some of them sunk into broken paving, others rolled across the forecourt into the lobby of the office, still others crashing through the stairway and the railings, all of them positioned with careful consideration.

Two large "craters" filled with water present a dramatic scene. Out of the water of each crater, a huge boulder rises up, only to crash back down again as though it had just come hurtling in from outer space. The smaller of the two emerges every 60 seconds, and sinks again immediately. The other one takes a whole hour to emerge before plunging back into the water with a crash.

This fascinating fountain, deceptive in its simplicity, required enormous technical expertise. Brunner, who always places particular value on technical perfection and fine craftsmanship, called in specialists to solve the problems of hydraulics (lifting and sinking the stones) and to calculate the water movement (outflow of water displaced by the sinking stones and pumping it back into the pool). The technical details, however, were only of secondary interest to the artist. His talent lies in integrating a wide variety of trades and skills in the implementation of his unusual ideas. The fact that the design differed considerably from the original concept was due to external circumstances.

As with most of Edy Brunner's work, it is difficult to classify the "Chempe" fountain, if at all. Is it land art, environmental design, concept art? This question has never interested him. Brunner is a conceptualist and generalist. His works – and this one in particular – offer a wealth of associative possibilities. He points out the relationship of stone to life itself (and to the VITA company name), and his fountain has been described as a rockfall or rockslide by both Franz Hohler and Dona Galli-Dejaco. Christoph Hackelsberger has likened "Chempe" to seedlings. It has been associated with catastrophe, with insecurity and modern society's need for insurance, and it has simply been described as a fountain. All these interpretations are possible, and the associations intended. It is this, together with the brilliant execution of the design, that determines the quality of a great work of art.

Literature:

Künstl. Schmuck VITA-Bürogebäude "Wieding". 1. Preis: Edy Brunner. In: Aktuelle Wettbewerbsszene. Schweizer Fachjournal für Architektur und Baudesign, Zürich, 4/5, 1978, p. 109 ff.

D.D.: Wenn "Chempe" tanzen … Neue Chancen für "Kunst am Bau" beim VITA-Neubau Zürich-Wieding. In: Der Bund, Bern, 15 July 1978, p. 29

Das Interview. Heute mit Edy Brunner, Schöpfer von CHEMPE. In: Blickpunkt Wieding 3. Zürich: VITA Versicherung, December 1978, p. 4 ff.

Die Vita auf dem Wiedinghügel. In: Neue Zürcher Zeitung, No. 265, 13 November 1980

Ein Felssturz in Wiedikon. In: Tages-Anzeiger, Zürich, 14 November 1980

Edy Brunner-Brunnen. In: Zürich-Gazette, 30/15 December 1980

Dona Galli-Dejaco: Felssturz – und wie man einen macht. In: Werk, Bauen + Wohnen, Zürich, 4/1981, p. 6 f.

Franz Hohler: Brunners Steinschlag. In: Weltwoche Magazin, Zürich, No. 32, 5 August 1981, p. 24 ff.

RDS: Mitten in Zürich: Steinschlag. Kaum ist der Platz fertig, da geht einer hin und zertrümmert die Arbeit wieder. In: Sonntags Zeitung, Zürich, 23 August 1981, p. 5

Christoph Hackelsberger: Findlinge-Setzlinge. Ein lapidarer Versuch künsterlischer Verfremdung. In: Süddeutsche Zeitung, No. 292, 19/20 December 1981

HM: Edi Brunners "Chempe". "Chempe" d'Edi Brunner. Edi Brunner's "Chempe": In: anthos, Zürich, 2/1982, p. 9 ff.

Rolf Lambrigger: Zürich. Zeitgenössische Kunstwerke im Freien. Zürich/Schwäbisch Hall: Orell Füssli Verlag, 1985, p. 256 f.

Chempe Jacket to Hang on a Nail

1980

Multiple
Jacket (size 54) of plastic film, photos, stones
Edition of 3

When Edy Brunner finished working on the "Chempe" fountain in front of the VITA insurance company headquarters in Zürich-Wieding, his largest environmental work to date, he wanted to mark the end of what had been a very important period for him. The idea of hanging your jacket on a nail at the end of a day's work, inspired by the great German comedian Karl Valentin who "hung his career on a nail" led him to create his special "Chempe Jacket".

He had three jackets tailored for him in transparent plastic film with one breast pocket and two side pockets. In the breast pockets he placed some black and white photos (9 x 13 cm) taken by Leonardo Bezzola during and after construction of the fountain. He placed small stones in the side pockets. The jacket could be presented on a coathanger. For the artist, it was the symbolic conclusion of a period of intensive work on the "Chempe" environment, a kind of valediction for himself.

4 Stones

1979

Multiple
1 pebble (from the Valle Maggia, Ticino) and 3 copies of the
stone in black, grey and white marble
Edition of 3

Edy Brunner's love of stone as a precious and versatile material
is evident throughout his work of the 70s and, time and time
again, it has inspired remarkable concepts and realizations. The
artist invariably draws his ideas from his own environment and
experience. In the Maggia valley in Ticino, where Brunner has
spent a lot of his time, he was fascinated by the pebbles in the
river. He admired their forms. Each one is unique and beautiful
in its own way.

Out of an immeasurable wealth of stones, he chose the
most beautiful for himself and then had three of them copied
mechanically in Carrara in white, grey and black marble (the
mixture of these colours resulting in the typical elegant grey of
the Maggia pebbles) to obtain four formally identical objects:
one original and three copies which could be produced in
unlimited quantities.

The fascinating aspect of a stone is its quiet beauty and its
uniqueness. The copies of the pebble, on the other hand, appear
elegant and noble, but they do not have the individuality of the
original that is the very essence of its value. The spectator, on
seeing the four stones for the first time, is immediately capti-
vated by the copies. Edy Brunner has set a trap for this attitude
by pricing the pebble very expensively and selling the marble
duplicates at cost price. The most valuable piece is the common
stone, for what are all the copies in the world, but for the original? In this way, the artist once again shows us a remarkable
aspect of our alienation from nature.

"Hast noch der Säulen ja"

1979

Environmental concept with fountain for an office building
in Bern-Beundenfeld
(competition design)

For his environments, Edy Brunner seeks points of departure in the existing situation, in existing materials or in special references to the planned location. None of them is conceivable at any other place than the one for which he designed it – for him there is no repetition. This also applies to his concept for the forecourt of an administrative building in Bern.

In this case, he was inspired by the stringently geometric pattern of pillars supporting the building. Brunner's idea was to continue this pattern onto the plaza in front of the building and use it as the basis for a pillar installation. The impression he planned to create was that of a "field of pillars" that had existed even before the construction of the office building; pillars embedded in the earth and covered with metal just waiting for the architect to draw those he needed for the building out of the ground.

On the plaza, the pattern was to be formed by partly and completely visible pillars and by the metal lids of those still embedded in the ground. The visible pillars were capped with metal and had a ring by which they could be pulled out of the ground. The pillars on the inside of the building were also to be given metal caps to link them clearly with those in the outdoor field of pillars and create a visual transition from inside to outside.

For the pillars on the plaza, Edy Brunner developed a number of different design variations. In addition to the metal lids embedded in the ground (representing pillars that had not been drawn out) and the partially and fully raised pillars, he planned a rolling landscape in which the pillars would disappear to some degree, and a "water pillar complex". These "water pillars" were to be outwardly identical to all the others, but would have a pipeline inside them carrying water to the top, which would then run down the outside of the pillar and disappear into the ground. Brunner had first used water as an element within a larger and more complex environment for his *"Quellhügel"* ("spring hill") at the Heuried housing project. In his first independent fountain for the VITA insurance company in Zürich-Wieding, he created a relationship between the inside of the building and the external environment. The concept of the pillar environment reveals a further component of Edy Brunner's creative output: underlining the work with a key that is a firm component of the concept. In this way, the work becomes a visualization of this key, just as other works by Brunner visualize concepts. The title *"Hast noch der Säulen ja"* ("You still have pillars" is an ironic reference to an old wartime song *"Hast noch der Söhne ja"* ("You still have sons").

Wassersäulen-
anlage

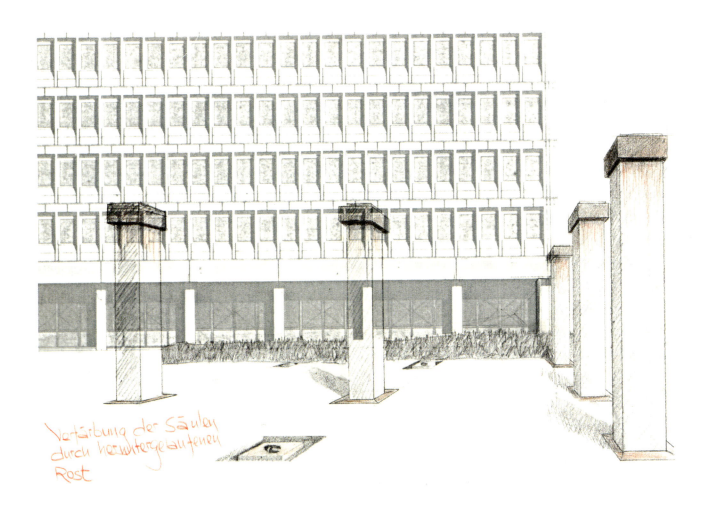

Verfärbung der Säulen
durch heruntergelaufenen
Rost

eine Hügellandschaft lässt
die Säulen zum Teil
"bis zum Hals" verschwinden ...

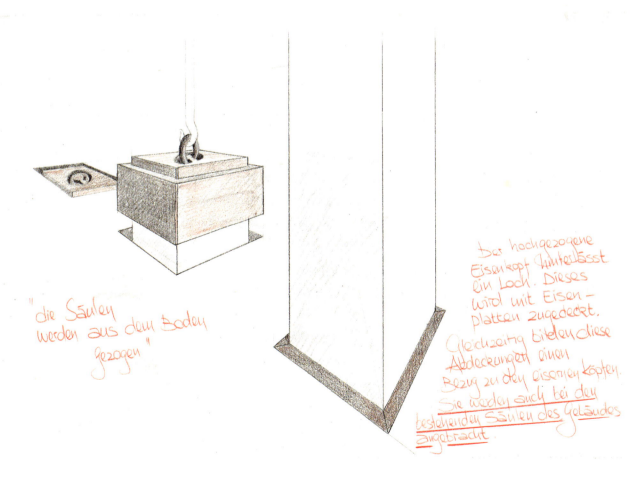

"die Säulen
werden aus dem Boden
gezogen"

Der hochgezogene
Eisenkopf hinterlässt
ein Loch. Dieses
wird mit Eisen-
platten zugedeckt.
Gleichzeitig bieten diese
Abdeckungen einen
Bezug zu den eisernen köpfen.
Sie werden auch bei den
bestehenden Säulen des Gebäudes
angebracht.

Molecular Fountain

1982–84

Environment with fountain at the head office of Serono S.A. in Aubonne

When Edy Brunner was invited to participate in the competition for an environment with fountain at the head office of Serono S.A. in Aubonne, he initially sought his starting point in the furniture for the planned cafeteria, inspiring him to design a "chair fountain" – the design with which he actually won the competition.

Brunner's concept envisaged selecting a tubular steel chair from the cafeteria and – based on the arrangement of the chairs – creating an installation using exactly the same tubular steel chairs, irregularly stacked and transformed into a system of water pipes. The chair arrangement was to be transformed almost imperceptibly into a kind of "chair chaos" and the dividing line between the chair as a functional object and the chair as a ready-made part of an unfunctional artistic installation was to be blurred. The chair installation transformed into a pipeline system was to be slowly flooded through many small apertures and holes (existing or created) until the basin is filled. At fixed time intervals, the water that had gathered was then to be released suddenly into a second empty basin from which it could then be pumped again slowly through the chair pipeline system into the first basin.

Edy Brunner was unable to persuade the client to accept this idea. The client felt that the chair was not an appropriate design element and that it bore no relation to the company's products (pharmaceuticals). The artist then spent an entire day visiting the company and being guided through its production works. He subsequently modified his project, abandoning the chair and, inspired by the laboratory installations, he simply designed a pipeline installation instead based on the principle of gradually flooding one basin and periodically emptying the water into a second basin.

He based this new concept on an invented legend: after completing the installation work in the building, the company finds that the assembly workers have made an error. The entire pipeline installation has to be torn out and is simply thrown in a heap in front of the building where it remains to this day, dripping. On this basis, Brunner arranged a kind of organized chaos of pipelines creating a self-contained system, whose similarity with micro-molecular structures inspired Franz Hohler to write his text *"Der Molekularsprengler"*. The pipes have had holes bored in them at several points so that the water spraying out of them gradually fills the basin and floods the installation. As the artist intended the fountain to function all year round, he had to take into account that it would freeze in winter and that

this could damage the pipeline system. The further apertures and tears through which water can escape and leak is not only tolerated as a natural factor, but is actually part of the intended individual (and quasi chaotic) concept designed by Edy Brunner.

Literature:

L. Bezzola: Umgebungsgestaltung mit Brunnenanlage in Aubonne VD. In: anthos, Zürich, 4/1986, p. 19

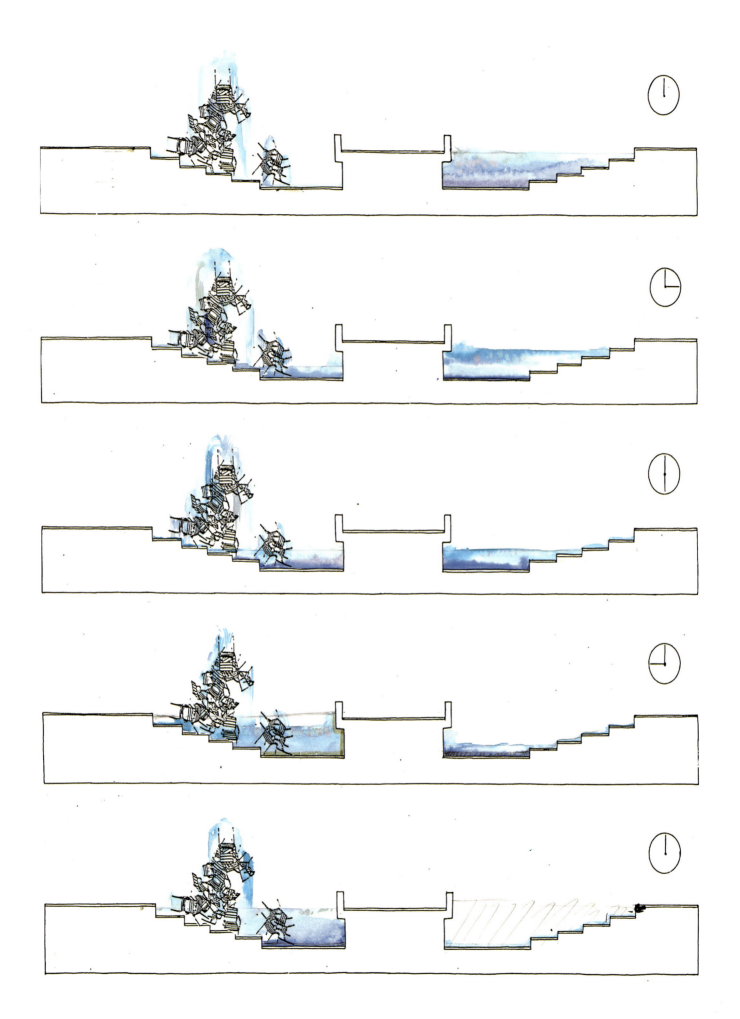

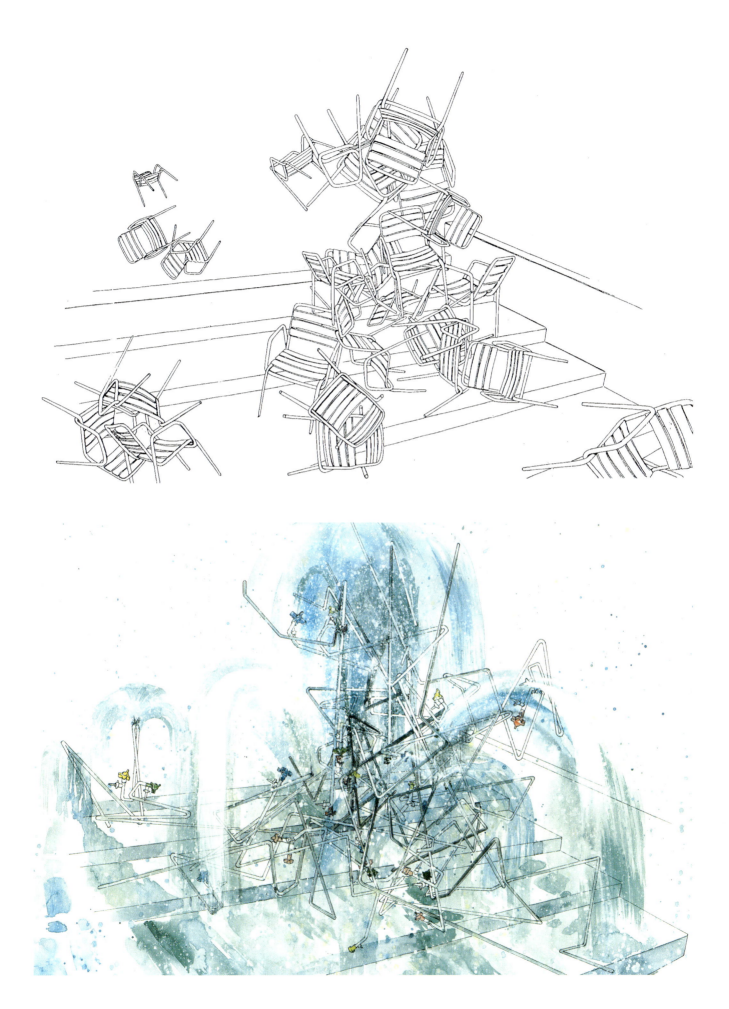

The Molecular Plumber
(Explaining a Fountain)

Once upon a time there was a plumber who studied molecular biology in his free time. Night after night he would try to discover the secret of human genetics, and soon he could think of little else.

This eventually started to affect his work. He began installing waterpipes with strangely winding forms and if anybody asked him about it, he would explain that amino acids also have a slightly twisted structure and that we owe our lives to them, as it were.

He could supply a u-bend with 36 indentations and if anybody asked him why, he would say, "Look, just one chromosome too many and you'll come into the world as an idiot."

Needless to say, this kind of attitude can soon put an end to a plumber's career.

What you are looking at here is an attempt to assemble the gas, water and oxygen pipes of a chemical laboratory as a disoxyribonucleine spiral, and the tragedy of that is that this work, this crowning glory of an ambitious chemist, should meet with the utter incomprehension of the client, who insisted that all he wanted was a his pipelines.

But for the fact that, on the very day on which the irate laboratory director had the whole lot thrown out, the artist Edy Brunner happened to stroll across the forecourt and made a fountain out of the ruins, we would now have one testament less to humankind's honourable quest for truth.

Franz Hohler (1984)

The Bridge of Biel .

1983

Environmental design for a secondary school in Biel
(competition design)

A design was sought for a plaza on the grounds of a new secondary school in Biel. The architecture is clear and functional. The area around the building has also been designed to harmonize with the architecture, providing considerable potential for further intervention. On the grassy areas, there are 1 x 1 m concrete slabs forming a regular geometric pattern that re-iterates the facades of the school building. For Edy Brunner, the most attractive part of the grounds was a small bridge over the Schüss stream at a point where the riverbed has been artificially straightened and breaks through the pattern of concrete slabs. It does not actually disturb the geometric pattern, but merely omits a certain number of grid elements.

Brunner's concept is based on this clearly defined situation. He exaggerates the existing situation, spinning it into a yarn that becomes a legend of the environment: *Human interven-tion goes one step further. The stone slabs, one metre square, encroach ominously upon the Schüss river from both sides, devouring the last blades of grass, spreading over the water to close in the area. The little river flows through its stony tunnel ... in Year X, nature strikes back. A catastrophic storm is un-leashed. The Schüss, its primordial powers restored, swells to a roaring flood, thundering through Biel carrying thousands of tons of stone and pebbles, tearing the plaza apart. Between the broken slabs that have fallen into the river, the water shoots up in fountains ... what is left is a heap of rubble, from which water continues to spray and ooze. In the cracks, green shoots begin to appear. But man hurriedly constructs a (tem-porary) wooden bridge to link the two banks.* (Brunner)

The intervention of the artist would have been restricted to arranging the scenario described, would have taken place on the banks of the little river and would not have had any disrup-tive influence whatsoever on the already completed grounds of the school. Brunner's idea referred to the one place he saw as requiring change: the perfectly straight channel through which the little river flows ("as though it were ashamed of its pathetic existence"). It involved staging the situation of a collapsed riverbank by using the existing concrete slabs and by installing a pump system that draws water out of the Schüss and sprays it out again through some jets positioned between the broken slabs. The (temporary) wooden bridge mentioned in the story already existed. Gradually, grass grew on the banks and created the situation described by Brunner.

This moment of chaos and catastrophe is a typical feature in the work of Edy Brunner. It is a deliberate aspect of confu-sion in an environment shaped by human society's exaggerated sense of security, order and cleanliness which can lead only to mediocrity. His relationship to primal forces, to the design elements of water and stone, to the arbitrary intervention of nature in art, is drawn from a profound distaste for all that is definitive and finished.

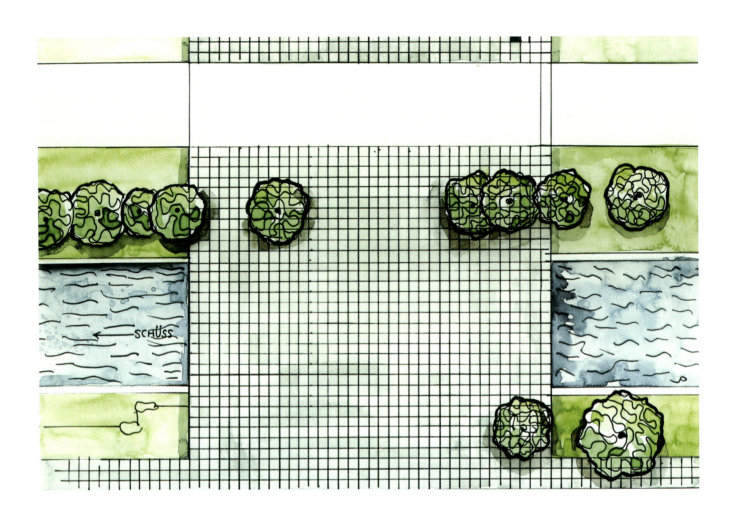

Page 68: imagined place

Page 69, top: storm damage

Page 69, bottom: project proposal

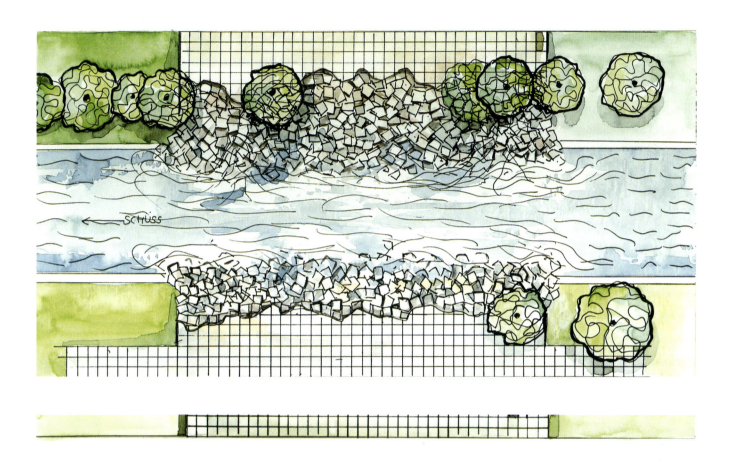

"Wasserspiegel"

20 June – 30 August 1986

Floating object on the river Limmat near the Münsterbrücke bridge as part of the 2000 year jubilee celebrations of the city of Zürich

9 Elements, 3 x 3 m each (81 m² in total), aluminium frame, polystyrene, plexiglass mirror

As part of the jubilee celebrations marking the 2000th anniversary of the city of Zürich, Edy Brunner was able to realize an extraordinary project. He planned an installation on the river Limmat and, in several steps, he developed the concept of the *"Wasserspiegel"*. A mirror made up of 9 segments, floating on the Limmat and anchored to the Münsterbrücke bridge, it is the external expression of a many-faceted artistic concept. His experience in environmental and exhibition design allowed him to implement this idea with ease, in spite of the many technical and organizational details involved in anchoring the object to the Münsterbrücke bridge in Zürich.

The *"Wasserspiegel"* has an important position amongst Brunner's many environments. With a hitherto unparalleled asceticism of means, the artist visualized a concept, wrenching it out of the context in which it is used in everyday language. In contrast to the other installations by this artist, this object is not immediately accessible to the spectator as a spatial or sensual experience. Although situated at one of the busiest points of the city, it was nevertheless remote and inaccessible, thus appearing as dematerialized as a vision and taking on a certain metaphysical aspect. Through his choice of time and place for the installation, Brunner achieved additional inspiration for a wide range of philosophical reflections far beyond the original intention of the work.

Mirror on the river, mirror amidst reflecting water, mirror of an idea. "Wasserspiegel", in German, means both "water mirror" and "water level", so that the title of the work actually refers to a measure of depth and to a reflection at the same time. Water levels, high or low, are everyday changes destined to be forgotten. Only the stonebuilt surroundings remain, built by those whose mirror images have long since been obliterated by the waves. The water that mirrored them has since flowed on and all that remains is their work, shaping the city. The image of today is to be captured, broken by the rise and fall of waves, recalling that history can be understood only in retrospect, and can only be fully grasped by the generations that follow in a broken form. Two thousand years seen through a mirror, within ourselves, reflecting for a moment, introverted, wondering "what is that down there on the Limmat?" These images that turn our familiar world inside out. Art as history.

(Albert Gyr, text on the invitation to the vernissage of the installation).

Literature:

(mf.): Spieglein, Spieglein in der Limmat ... In: Zürifäscht. (Supplement). Zürich: Verkehrsverein, 1986, p. 2

(thas): Des Grossmünsters Grimassen in der Limmat. In: Tages-Anzeiger, Zürich, 2 July 1986

Der Landbote, Zürich, 2 July 1986, p. 21

Luzerner Neueste Nachrichten, Luzern, 2 July 1986

Tagblatt der Stadt Zürich, Zürich, 2 July 1986, p. 1

(sda): Ein "Wasserspiegel" auf der Limmat. In: Neue Zürcher Zeitung, 3 July 1986, p. 46

(sda): Ein "Wasserspiegel" schwimmt auf der Limmat. In: Zürichsee-Zeitung, Zürich, 3 July 1986, p. 5

(c): 2000 Jahre Stadt Zürich spiegeln sich in der Limmat. In: Der Bund, Bern, 5 July 1986, p. 7

Altstadt Kurier, Zürich, 15 July 1986, p. 4

Willy Rotzler: 25 Jahre Kunst in der Schweiz. In: das kunstwerk, Stuttgart, 39. Jg., 4-5/September 1986, ill. p. 28

Walter Stampa: Edy Brunner, Künstler und Gestalter. In: EXPO DATA, Zürich, 4 (April)/1992, p. 24 ff.

Apple Music Box

1987

Video environment concept
In collaboration with Francesco Mariotti

In 1979, Edy Brunner designed an exhibition stand for the Swiss national tourist office and, in 1986, he was commissioned to draw up a study for a touring exhibition. The idea was that an exhibition container system should tour a number of cities to carry out advertising campaigns there. For the study, Edy Brunner called upon his colleague Francesco Mariotti, with whom he developed the concept of an unconventional multimedia exhibition environment which was, unfortunately, never executed.

Based on the fact that the first music boxes were made 200 years ago by Jaquet-Droz in the Swiss Jura, Edy Brunner and Francesco Mariotti decided to pick up where this pioneering invention left off and combine it with state-of-the-art mechanical, electronic and audiovisual technology. The artists came up with the spherical form of a 5 metre high apple made of a special material (granite or similar, with the possibility of fitting solar cells on the outside) to create a 7 part video environment as the basis for artistic activities.

Accompanied by specially written music box compositions, 6 apple segments can be driven out to a distance of 5 metres. The core of the apple remains in the form of a 6 part video wall with 54 monitors in the centre, while the segments moving out turn towards the spectators. Each segment has 9 monitors superimposed in a row. The spectator can enter the apple. The 54 core monitors screen an animation programme supported by the images, sound and light effects of the moving apple segments.

Computer technology allows each monitor to be separately controlled. Various compositions of stills and moving images or live images are possible. Acoustic and visual changes in the environment are fed into the system via sensors. The alters the light and sound programme of the apple, creating astonishing effects which emphasize the playful element and actively involve the spectator in the event. Live cultural events (ballet, concerts, pantomime etc.) can also use these (extended) choreographic possibilities. It is also conceivable that programmes can be created by various artists specially for the video monitors of the apple. The 7 part apple environment may thus be regarded as a kind of hardware for which a wide variety of software versions are possible.

The Apple Music Box could be used to carry a cultural message on tour to major cities in Europe and overseas. The exhibition venues would be busy hubs in international centres. The apple environment with its modern technology and performances by groups of artists would attract attention as a spectacle and an attraction. The actual information, however, would be passed on by word of mouth. For this reason, the Apple Music Box would be accompanied by information containers where person to person talks could take place. These independent information units could be set up anywhere or, depending on the situation, only in certain countries. The apple motif should appear everywhere: from small give-aways to promotional articles for sale.

The basic structure of the environment is, of course, also suitable as a vehicle for purely technical (commercial) information, for example at industrial exhibitions and trade fairs. The unusual spherical form of the installation would probably be a real crowd-puller at an industrial exhibition. Cultural fringe programmes would also be possible. Finally, the Apple Music Box could be installed as a stationary environment or as part of a prestigious architectural project (lobby etc.). In such a case, a multi-functional usage would also be possible: as an environment with a purely artistic character, as a vehicle for advertising and promotion, and as a medium for which other artists could be invited to develop concepts.

Literature:

Swiss Music Box. Attraktive Schweiz-Werbung. Zürich: Schweizerische Verkehrszentrale (SVZ), 1987

Granite Apple

1987

Musical object
In collaboration with Francesco Mariotti
Granite, metal, music box mechanism
H: 33 cm, Ø 28 cm

While they were working on the design of the Apple Music Box, Brunner and Mariotti took the concept of the mobile video environment of a granite-skinned apple one step further. They designed a music box in the form of an apple made of granite inside which they installed a music box mechanism produced in St. Croix, to be switched on and off by pressing the funnel-shaped stem of the apple. This object was intended to be produced in a large edition as a gift for sponsors of the Apple Music Box.

Brunner and Mariotti also considered producing a special music box multiple for all locations where the Apple Music Box environment was installed, involving a composer and an artist from the respective region. The composer would create a piece of music for the music box and the artist would design the shell. These multiples would be sold and would also be shown in a special exhibition at the end of the tour.

Water Birds

1991

Swan, seagull, duck, wagtail, diver
5 kinetic objects
In collaboration with Francesco Mariotti

Prototype model

At the end of 1989, the district of Horgen began making its initial plans for the 700th anniversary celebrations of the Swiss Federation in 1991. They adopted the motto "Läbe und Schaffe am See" (living and working by the lake), but were unable to find a common concept for the artistic expression of the theme. In the end, Edy Brunner came up with his idea of modern, interactive, mobile art objects. Together with Francesco Mariotti, he presented the concept of a "fantastic symphony for an industrial orchestra".

The concept is a perfect symbiosis of the design intentions of both artists. Life by the lake is symbolized by five technoid, kinetic sculptures of various types of birds normally found by Lake Zürich: swan, seagull, duck, wagtail and diver. Brunner developed the overall artistic concept, while Mariotti worked on the form and function of the objects. In doing so, he was able to call upon his previous experience in creating techno-zoomorphic sculptures, strongly abstracted animal shapes with various multimedia, electronically controlled functions.

The objects are abstracted representations of the five types of birds mentioned. Each object has three pairs of wings, and the six ends of these are mobile. Solar cells installed on the upper side of the wings power batteries which drive all the electronic functions: spraying water, moving wings, lighting, making music, switching on and off by sensors. For each type of bird, a special electronic music was composed and recorded to reflect the habits and voices of the birds on three different tracks (rhythm, atmosphere, cry) played through one pair of wings.

For a procession on 7 July 1991, the objects were mounted on mobile bases made of converted and disguised cars. After the procession, Brunner and Mariotti created a spacious installation on a meadow of the Au peninsula by Lake Zürich for the period from 30 August to 8 September 1991. A path led along one side of the meadow. Each visitor walking along the path triggered the built-in sensors, making the models function and thus becoming an integral part of the "fantastic symphony for an industrial orchestra".

Literature:

Peter H. Blattmann: Wie es zu unserer Stelze kam. In: häsch g'hört. Corporate periodical for the staff of Blattmann & Co AG, Wädenswil, No. 69/Winter 1991, p. 36 ff.

Photography

Photogram

1964/65

The inevitable and frequently monotonous darkroom work of a photographic retoucher inevitably led Edy Brunner to experiment and create photograms. However, in doing so, he did not simply arrange a variety of objects on photographic paper and then expose the paper, but worked instead entirely with the light of the enlarger which he modulated either by hand or using specially made frames, creating pure "luminograms"*). He manipulated the lenses of the enlarger so that each object caught in the ray of light appeared distorted on the exposed surface. After a number of experiments in which he created figures arbitrarily by hand, resulting in free images, he developed a sequence systematically shadowing the ray of light with forms and creating increasingly complex configurations of a serial character.

In order to underline the production process, involving the manipulation of light and the resulting shadows, Brunner exposed negative film so that the light parts appear light on the paper enlargements while the shadow parts appear dark. He made the reproducibility of these works an integral part of the concept by declaring the paper prints to be originals (and the exposed negatives as a mere interim phase). This a very early indication of his affinity to the serially manufactured product and clearly expresses his rejection of the cult of the unique work of art.

Notes:

*) See: Floris M. Neusüss / Renate Heyne (Mitarb.): Das Fotogramm in der Kunst des 20. Jahrhunderts. Die andere Seite der Bilder – Fotografie ohne Kamera. Cologne: DuMont Buchverlag, 1990, p. 482

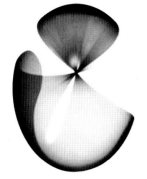

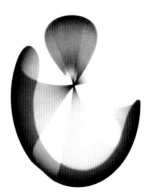

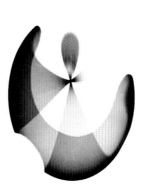
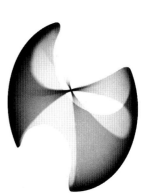

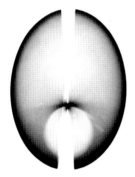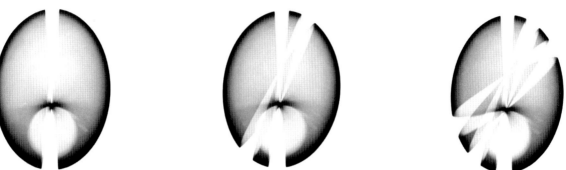

At the latest since the publication of his book *"viewpoint"* in 1987, Edy Brunner's panorama photos have been in the public eye. The book contains photographs taken 1983 on a number of journeys. Edy Brunner first began to take an interest in panorama photography as a medium when he saw the work of the Munich-based photographer Klaus Kinold for the first time in 1981. He had known Kinold since 1978 when they both lived in a converted spaghetti factory in Ticino. Brunner was impressed by the extremely high quality of the prints and by the elongated format (proportional ratio 1:3) to which he had a strong affinity and which also forms the basis of other creative works by him. He discussed the technical and aesthetic problems of panorama photography with Kinold and, in 1982, he purchased his first panorama camera.

In the spring of 1982, Kinold and Brunner went on a photo tour together in the mountains of Ticino. Since then, Edy Brunner has used the panorama camera on his travels. In 1985, in order to further consolidate his knowledge of photography, he took part in a workshop run by Peter Gasser for the black and white photography in which he has specialized. His experiments with colour panorama photography, as documented for example in *"viewpoint"*, were soon abandoned in favour of exploring the possibilities of black and white panorama photography and in pursuit of his own original way of seeing.

In spite of its wide angle of 90°, panorama photography offers the photographer a relatively limited range of design possibilities: wide format images of natural or urban landscapes or still life arrangements. In pursuit of the creative mastery of this extremely elongated format, the most logical approach would seem to be a symmetrical structure emphasizing the centre. This is the approach chosen by Edy Brunner. Moreover, a camera with an undistorted viewfinder creates the added difficulty of making the image appear in a way that is not quite identical to the image recorded on the film, calling for considerable experience in handling the camera. As a result, composition takes place directly before the subject. Brunner

eschews any subsequent manipulations beyond the scope of minor corrections. He generally photographs standing up to reflect the human gaze.

Edy Brunner does not make the silver prints on Agfa paper himself. In order to achieve the standards of quality he demands, Edy Brunner entrusts the printing to a friend, the Cologne-based photographer Susanne Trappmann. Thanks to her long-standing collaboration with Klaus Kinold, she is thoroughly familiar with the problems of panorama photography. Edy Brunner invariably discusses the selection of photos with her as well as the qualitative details and he also listens willingly to her advice, for he respects her craftsmanship and her judgement.

A comparison of his works dating from the period 1983–90 clearly shows that, wherever Edy Brunner takes his photographs, he composes them around the centre of the image. This design approach is so strongly evident that the similarity between widely divergent subjects can be quite remarkable. His photos soon gained technical perfection and brilliance and the sophisticated compositions began to betray a certain mannered style, due to the fact that Brunner invariably selects his subjects on the basis of creative aspects alone.

In the spring of 1990, for an exhibition in Halle an der Saale, someone suggested to Edy Brunner that he should create a major series of such photos taken in a single place over a long period of time: in Dresden. He took up the idea and, in May 1990, he visited the historic city on the river Elbe for the first time. He was immediately fascinated by the distinctive atmosphere of the city. Following his instinct, he began moving around the city aimlessly, in search of interesting subjects.

He initially avoided the temptations of the touristic "sightseeing eye", preferring to look behind the scenes of the city and capture a mood that was likely to escape those visiting the town only briefly. With the aid of Matthias Griebel, who has a thorough knowledge of Dresden and its history, he was able to establish an increasingly intimate rapport with the city and its

environs. Gradually, he began to approach the more famous sights, finding new angles and alienating them in his photos in his own inimitable way. By the time he had finished working on this series in March 1991, he had created more than 750 photos, of which he selected 167 for printing. This colelction constitutes his largest and most significant series of panorama photos to date. While he was working on the series, Brunner's compositional principles became increasingly distinctive. In addition to symmetrical visual structures, he also created photos which succeeds in achieving a delicate balance of pictorial elements beyond considerations of symmetry and without any obvious visual "arrangement".

Edy Brunner's panorama photographs since 1983 can be broken down into 19 major groups of works, most of them created on his travels: Teneriffa (1983/1985); Ticino (1984–89); USA (1984/1991/92); Florida (1986); Maine (1987); Chicago/Lake Michigan (1989); Lanzarote (1985); Crete (1985); Tuscany (1986); Moscow (1987); Stockholm (1987); GDR (1988–91); East and West-Berlin (1988); Carribbean (1988); Portugal (1989–92); Netherlands (1989); La Palma (1990/91); Dresden (1990/91); Entlebuch (1991); Schweizerischer Turnertag, Lucerne (1991); Portrait (since 1984); Nude (1992).

Literature:

Edy Brunner: viewpoint. (With a foreword by Willy Rotzler and essays by Franz Hohler). Zürich: ABC-Verlag, 1987

Peter Pachnicke: Berückende und rätselhafte Fremdheit. In: Neue Berliner Illustrierte, Berlin (East), No. 28/1989, p. 23

Hans-Georg Sehrt: Fotos aus dem Plaste-Ei. Edy-Brunner-Ausstellung in der Galerie Roter Turm. In: Mitteldeutsche Neueste Nachrichten, Halle, 7 April 1990

Hans-Georg Sehrt: Eigenwilliges eines Schweizer Fotografen. In: Mitteldeutsche Zeitung, Halle, 10 May 1990, p. 5

F. Reinke: Die Faszination der Stille. In: Tribüne, Berlin (East), 17 April 1990

Christina Sitte: Sehen, Erkennen, Photographieren. Beachtenswertes Kunstschaffen in den Kleinstädten. In: Die Synthese, Zürich, No. 239/ December 1991, p. 1·1

Dresden. Panoramafotografien von Edy Brunner. (Calendar 1993. With a text in German by Axel Wendelberger). Ditzingen und Gotha: Grafisches Zentrum Drucktechnik, 1992

24. Internationaler Fotokalender-Preis. In: PROFIFOTO, Düsseldorf, 2 (March/April)/1993, p. 49 ff.

DRESDEN. Panoramafotografien 1990/91 von Edy Brunner. (With a foreword by Matthias Griebel and an essay by Axel Wendelberger. In German). Schaffhausen: Edition Stemmle, 1993

DRESDEN. Panoramafotografien 1990/91. (Portfolio of 30 original photographs by Brunner. With a text in German by Grit Wendelberger). Düsseldorf: Galerie Neumann, 1993

Genia Bleier: Ein Schweizer entdeckt Dresden. In: Dresdener Neueste Nachrichten, 11/12 September 1993

Konrad Hirsch: Dresden zwischen Verharren und Hoffnung. Panoramafotografien von Edy Brunner im Stadtmuseum. In: Dresdener Neueste Nachrichten, 14 September 1993

Klaus Sebastian: Jagdschlösser, stille Elbdampfer und Trabis. In: Rheinische Post, No. 13

MGM: Spaziergänge mit der Kamera. Dresden – aus der Sicht des Fotokünstlers Edy Brunner. In: Neue Rhein-Zeitung, 15 January 1994

Page 94:
Key West, Florida, USA. 1986

Page 95:
Courtyard of Dresden Palace. 1990

St. Lucia, Carribbean. 1988

Entlebuch, Switzerland. 1991

Dresden. 1990

Red Square, Moscow. 1987

Near Antequera, Spain. 1992

Monchique, Portugal. 1992

Near Antequera, Spain. 1992

Torrenieri, Tuscany. 1986

It's late, said the older cypress tree to the others, I think we should go. But when they turned around, they were startled.
Many things had changed.
Ah, she said, maybe we had better stay together a bit longer.

Franz Hohler (In "viewpoint", 1987)

Artist Wolfgang Mattheuer at Altes Museum, Berlin. 1988

Franz Hohler, Grit Wendelberger, Axel Wendelberger, Matthias Griebel and Edy Brunner at Dresden. (Automatic photo). 3 October 1990

Seattle, Washington, USA. 1993

Crater Lake, Oregon, USA. 1993

Sagres, Portugal. 1988

Near Leipzig. 1988

Serpa, Portugal. 1988

Guimaraes, Portugal. 1991

Rockland, Maine, USA. 1987

Riveo, Valle Maggia, Switzerland. 1984

"Triton's Gondola", built c. 1800, Schlossgarten Pillnitz near Dresden. 1990

Anhalter Bahnhof memorial, Berlin. 1988

Jacksonville, Oregon, USA. 1993

Rockland, Maine, USA. 1987

Dresden-Neustadt. 1990

Bath, Maine, USA. 1987

Design

Design

Edy Brunner has worked as a freelance designer since 1968, with the main emphasis on exhibition design. In this, as in all his creative work, it is the task itself that appeals to him. Here, too, he is inspired by the given situation, using the ordinary as the basis on which to develop something extraordinary. His experience in the field of fine art has been a fertile influence on his work as a designer. While the client's brief calls for utmost efficiency and precision, exhibition design being a keenly competitive sector, his forays into the world of art give him the necessary freedom of thought and playful approach that enable him to find unconventional solutions time and time again. This has brought him a reputation as one of Switzerland's most interesting exhibition designers, and one whose name is invariably mentioned "whenever there is talk of outstanding trade fair stands, and particularly prestigious trade fair presentations".*

Although Brunner has worked as a designer since going freelance, the path he has pursued has has not been entirely straightforward and his design output invariably has to be regarded in the light of his artistic output. Only by way of comparison with each other can his work in the fields of fine and applied arts be properly understood. The intellectual techniques involved in handling ideas and developing concepts are similar; experience in one field enhances his work in the other.

Edy Brunner's development as a designer has been shaped in particular by his work for one major client, Dow Chemical Europe S.A., an American chemicals producer whose European head office is in Switzerland. Dow Chemical's trade fair image was aimed at demonstrating that they were different and drawing attention by means of unusual trade fair stands and appearances. An aggressive sales policy coupled with considerable freedom for employee initiative also meant that the designer was given a fairly free rein. For Brunner, this was an ideal situation in which to tap his rich creative vein and cultivate his handling of form. Brunner has designed some of his finest trade fair stands for Dow Chemical, and this is due in no small part to the fact that he was fully aware of the company philosophy – and consequently knew what was expected of the designer – and also because the relevant members of staff placed enormous confidence in him.

Drawing attention by being different is a fundamental principle of Brunner's work as an exhibition designer. Visual competition amongst the stands at a trade fair is considerable. Exhibition design, like any other field, tends to follow fashions and the personal achievement of the designer is not always clearly recognizable. Brunner's strength in this respect is the fact that he invariably moved against the trend, reacting to the latest fashions by deliberately ignoring them and thereby automatically differing from his rivals. When the others opened up their stands and made them more transparent, Brunner created closed stands and little hall-within-a-hall structures. When stands became increasingly fantastic, he turned to architectonic principles, and the more emphasis was placed on design, the more he distanced himself from it, reducing his creations to the barest structural necessities and following the laws of computer-backed manufacturing processes.

In order to accommodate the requirements of a variety of clients, it is not enough to simply stand out from the crowd by producing extraordinary design concepts. Economic viability is also an important factor. One way in which Brunner achieves this is by reducing the design input. What is more, he acts as general contractor and is therefore responsible not only for the design of the stands, but also for their construction. In this way, he is in charge of the entire production process and can influence it at any stage, thereby achieving a high degree of efficiency. His vast experience and professional competence in this field allowed him, as sole contractor, to complete the Swiss Pavilion for the 1991 Geneva Telecom, the world's biggest telecommunications fair, to within SF 10 of the client's budget of SF 2.5 million.

Brunner, however, does not simply choose his contracts according to the budget involved. He has also come up with some interesting designs for smaller clients. Generally speaking, the task itself has to interest him. In 1970, for example, he designed the Munich boutique "Up to Date"** on a shoe-string budget, using galvanized fencing wire throughout the black saleroom as a structural component, as a decorative element and as clothes stands. In 1992, he designed the interior of a Düsseldorf gallery. Fixtures and furniture were produced in clear varnished sheet metal, giving the impression of raw metal.

The writing tables and reception are fitted with black lacquered fiberboard. It is the reduction to geometric forms that enhances the aesthetic value of the objects. No unnecessary detail has been added; everything is restricted to functional, structural and production necessities.

Even his most sophisticated trade fair stands are based on this principle. He invariably reveals the technical and structural framework so that the architecture is clearly legible. Indeed, in his most recent works, he highlights only the technical structure of the stands and no longer places the design within the construct of a basic idea, such as the visualization of concepts evident in "Le Breakthrough" (1982), but concentrates instead on the presentational function alone, as in "Dachlandschaft/ Roofscape" (1990).

This latest trend in Brunner's work as a designer also reflects his increasing awareness of environmental and ecological responsibility. His choice of the appropriate material for the task, his minimalistic approach to building and perhaps even his abandonment of colour may be regarded not only as the credo of this designer's impressive 25-year progress in design, but also as Edy Brunner's response to the ever-changing and increasingly complex challenges of our times.

Literature:

* Walter Stampa: Edy Brunner, Künstler und Gestalter. In: EXPO DATA, Zürich, 4/1992, p. 24

** Wolfgang Grub: Boutiquen, Shops und schicke Läden. Munich: Verlag Georg Callwey, 1974, p. 64 f.

Incontro, Bern

1970
Home furnishings store

In collaboration with Remo Galli and Thomas Kühne

Literature:

shopping by ... incontro. In: modernes wohnen. schweizer zeitschrift für internationales wohnen. Zumikon, No. 41 / 71 (13. Jg., 1971), p. 29 ff.

Wolfgang Grub: Boutiquen, Shops und schicke Läden. Internationale Beispiele verkaufsfördernd gestaltet. Munich: Verlag Georg D.W. Callwey, 1974, p. 48 f.

Karl and Eva Mang: Neue Läden. Stuttgart: Verlag Gerd Hatje, 1981, p. 114 f.

Edy Brunner's first major design contract was for the interior of the *Incontro* home furnishings store in the historic centre of Bern. Working in collaboration with architects Remo Galli and Thomas Kühne, his interior design for the premises on three floors (ground floor and first floor sales room, second floor store room; width between 1.25 and 4 m, length 25 m) focused primarily on retaining the character of the historic building. No alterations were made to the original structure of the room. Steel beams were fitted to permit variations in the saleroom ceiling design. Fittings were reduced to a few simple and versatile components such as mobile wall elements, rolling shelf units and an open goods lift.

While Remo Galli and Thomas Kühne sought architectural solutions to questions of spatial organization, Edy Brunner turned his attention to the design features. To permit versatility in the presentation of the goods on sale, he developed an extremely simple mobile shelving system with back-lighting that would set highlights within the room as well as enhancing the glassware on display. Another interesting design element was the open goods lift serving all three floors which also could also be used to display a variety of objects. It was flanked to the right and left by tall, slim radiators.

For the outside of the store, Edy Brunner used a versatile system of narrow red polyester partition wall elements, slanted at irregular angles to one another and with large window apertures. These could be adjusted as required and in summer the entire area could be opened up. There was no display front in the conventional sense. The entrance to the shop was firmly installed between these walls. The door was operated by a sensor, opening automatically with the hydraulic mechanism of a tram door and giving the characteristic hissing sound of a tram door instead of the conventional shop bell.

The tension created between the ultra modern entrance and display area with its magnificent, formally reduced fittings, and the historical atmosphere of the unaltered stone walls, gave this shop its distinctive atmosphere. Functionality and sales promotion were the driving force behind the design concept. The objects on display were the decisive factor, and everything was geared towards their presentation. No superfluous design elements distracted the shopper's attention.

Smaller Stands 1970–1982

"Forest Stand" for Dow Chemical Europe S.A.
1970, Leipzig Autumn Fair

Brunner's first contract for Dow Chemical was not aimed at presenting a particular product, but at underlining the presence of one of the world's foremost plastics manufacturers at Leipzig trade fair, one of the leading industrial fairs in the Eastern Bloc. He projected the stand as a green forest made of plastics. As in his art works of this period, a distinct sense of conceptual humour is also evident here. The obvious contradiction in terms evoked by a plastic forest filled with the distorted sounds of taped birdsong created an absurd atmosphere, situating this installation within the highly charged terrain between (intentionally critical) art and the (affirmative) presentation of a chemical company, while successfully avoiding the pitfall of the unsubtle advertising gimmick.

Literature:

Hans Peter Held: Die Freiheit des Designers, Ausstellungskonzepte für Dow Chemical Europe S.A.. In: NOVUM Gebrauchsgraphik. Munich, 12 (December)/1973, p. 23

Stand for Dow Chemical Europe S.A.
1971, Pro Aqua – Pro Vita, Basel

The theme of the stand was the presentation of products for water treatment. White shop dummies were distributed over the darkened exhibition area, and moving coloured light was projected onto them to create the impression of flowing dirty water. In an open safe in the centre of the stand stood a glass of pure, clean water in a spotlight, presented as a precious exhibition item. A loudspeaker emitted a constant background sound of flowing water. Mirrored slanting walls gave the edges of the room a flowing aspect.

Literature:

Hans Peter Held: Die Freiheit des Designers, Ausstellungskonzepte für Dow Chemical Europe S.A.. In: NOVUM Gebrauchsgraphik. Munich, 12 (December)/1973, p. 18

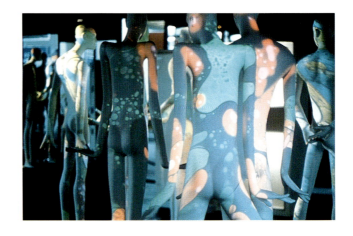

Stand for Dow Chemical Europe S.A.
1974, Constructa, Hanover

Dow Chemical has regularly presented polystyrene foam as an insulating material at building industry fairs. Edy Brunner created a number of different presentation approaches for this. For the Dow Chemical stand at the 1974 Constructa, he designed the stand ceiling using interlocking polystyrene foam slabs.

Stand for Dow Chemical Europe S.A.
1975, Deubau, Essen

A typical feature of the various approaches used by Brunner to present polystyrene foam at the Dow Chemical stands is the way he places the product above the normal field of vision of the visitor to create an optimum distance effect. At the stand for the 1975 Deubau, he used several Plexiglas pillars around which slabs of the material seem to "float" and which also serve as transparent carriers of information.

Stand for Oxy
1975, International Boat Exhibition, Paris

For the presentation of nautical equipment, Edy Brunner designed a stand for the Oxy company at the 1975 International Boat Exhibition in Paris using dark, deep-drawn plastic elements which subtly evoked a high-tech atmosphere. They provided information on the productions in a variety of ways, such as printed messages, slides or integrated monitors.

Stand for Dow Chemical Europe S.A.
1981, SPCI, Stockholm

The stands designed by Edy Brunner for Dow Chemical for the SPCI, the international paper fairs in Stockholm, were similar in appearance in that he had the information printed on lengths of paper affixed in various ways to presentation walls, with large strips of adhesive tape, with magnets or, in 1981, with over-sized paper clips.

Stand for Dow Chemical Europe S.A.
1982, Constructa, Hanover

At the 1982 Constructa, Dow Chemical once again presented polystyrene foam as an insulating material. For this, Edy Brunner designed tilted model stands topped with mirrors to duplicate and extend the perspective. The ceiling was made of insulating slabs in original size. For this, Edy Brunner designed large stands to which vertical lengths of polystyrene foam were attached like slats, giving the optical effect of a solid body, and visible from a considerable distance in spite of the relatively small size of the stand, thereby emphasizing the product.

Stand for the Swiss Tourist Board (SVZ)

1980, ITB Berlin
(International Tourism Fair)

The aim of standing out from the crowd inspired Edy Brunner to create a stand where everything would be "authentic", without creating a the kind of nostalgically kitschy atmosphere so often found at exhibitions in the tourism sector. The stand was divided into three sections according to the basic functions it had to fulfil: an exhibition area for information and public relations, a business area for meetings, and a restaurant for relaxation. All three functionally different parts were united under one roof and designed according to function: the exhibition area was open and transparent, the business area took the form of black niches sheltered from view, while the restaurant looked like a typical "Schweizer Beizli".

The "Restaurant Suisse" was a point of attraction and the focal point of the stand, and has been used repeatedly since then (in slightly modified form) by the Swiss National Tourist Board at its trade fairs. In Brunner's own words, "I wanted to use quality and authenticity to show what it is that makes Switzerland different..." and this is particularly true of the "Beizli". Everything was made of original materials. From the furniture to the matchboxes, from coffee to full meals – everything was specially delivered from Switzerland. In this way, he succeeded in creating a *"gemütlich"* and authentic atmosphere free of all pretence. He also avoided creating an isolated situation by leaving the ceiling open to provide a view of the roof structure.

Brunner designed the roof of the stand as a lightweight aluminium structure, its lightweight tubes supported by four outer pillars situated at the very edge of the designated stand area. Together with the engineer Peter Osterwalder, he created a special modular system of interlocking aluminium tubes with cube-shaped links. The ends of the tubes ran into steel-core strips bent at an angle of 45°. This system meant that an extremely stable yet light framework could be assembled quickly and easily, spanning an area of 27 x 9 m (243 m²). A simple textile covering formed a tent-like roof evoking a holiday atmosphere and reminiscent of the Swiss mountains. At the same time, it visually linked all the sections of the stand.

Versatile Exhibition System for Trade Fairs

1981

Independent

In order to be able to respond more quickly and adaptably to the needs of his clients, particularly Dow Chemical, Edy Brunner set about designing an exhibition system for trade fairs. This system is compellingly simple, easy to build and offers a huge range of individual design variations.

Made entirely of aluminium, it consists of only a few individual parts, which can be quickly assembled, disassembled and transported. Lightweight supports, designed according to a modular principle of lengths of 3/3, 2/3 and 1/3, form a framework system into which walls, display boards etc. can be fitted with ease. Sheet metal panels are slotted into the supporting framework and anchored by clamps, creating the outer shell for containers. In public areas (presentation and meeting areas) the walls can be covered in textiles. The lighting sytem is integrated into the ceiling structure of narrow strips. Originally in pure aluminium, the system was later anodized in the Dow Chemical corporate blue and also used in other colours.

Edy Brunner's design is much easier to assemble than most other conventional exhibition systems. It consists of only a few easy-to-handle components and, because it is so light, it can even be transported and effortlessly assembled by just one person. A complete small stand (a 3/3 cube with sides of 2,5 m) weighs between 30 and 50 kg. Brunner's system is also eye-catchingly different, as the stands appear relatively self-contained.

This exhibition system was used was for the first time to build the technical extensions for the "Le Breakthrough" stand for Dow Chemical at the 1982 Interplas fair in Paris. The first complete stand to be built by Brunner using only this system was for the Dow Chemical presentation at the 1983 Bowboers in Utrecht. Edy Brunner's exhibition system, which he has already applied in more than 100 different ways, offers a wide range of possible variations, from a simple, self-contained cube to a large, two-storey unit with an open floor plan. In this respect, he accommodates not only the needs and requirements of the exhibitor, but also responds to the given situation in each trade fair hall. Relatively small stands with a simple unit structure (SPCI 84 and 87 in Stockholm and Interpack 86 in Düsseldorf) can be set up quickly and easily even on a small budget. Even for stands involving a more complex structure of interlinked cubes (Bowboers 83 in Utrecht, Constructa 86 in Hanover and Huhn und Schwein 87 in Hanover) no great technical effort or financial expense is needed to create a spacious impression. The system also offers versatility in the layout of the individual units. In this way, the stands can be built to fit in with the trade fair hall (Pakex 86 in Birmingham).

Further individual variations and adaptation to suit the respective trade fair are also possible in the external design of the stands. For example, printed fabric can be spanned inside the structural framework as an advertising medium (Bowboers 83 in Utrecht) or individual fields can be filled out with figurative corporate identity figures as an eye-catcher (Huhn und Schwein 87 in Hanover). Brunner has also frequently used special trailers as optical highlights for product presentation and information, giving the stands a highly distinctive character (Interpack 84 in Düsseldorf, Pakex 86 in Birmingham or Constructa 86 in Hanover). In each case, there is clearly a wide range of possibilities, allowing a single exhibition system to be used over a long period for different individual projects. In this way, Brunner has succeeded in giving Dow Chemical a corporate image projection throughout Europe over the years at its trade fair visits, while avoiding the pitfall of monotony and boredom. Even today, Edy Brunner continues to design small stands on the basis of his own exhibition system, and invariably finds new and interesting design variations. Even for large individual trade fair stands, Brunner continues to use components of this system to create smaller containers.

Page 122:
Stand for Dow Chemical, Bowboers, Utrecht, 1983

Page 123, top:
Stand for Dow Chemical, Interpack, Düsseldorf, 1984

Page 123, bottom:
Stand for Dow Chemical, SPCI, Stockholm, 1984

Pages 124/125:
Stand for Dow Chemical, Constructa, Hanover, 1986

Page 126:
Stand for Dow Chemical, Pakex, Birmingham, 1986

Page 127:
Stand for Dow Chemical, Huhn und Schwein, poultry and pigmeat fair, Hanover, 1987

Pages 128/129:
Stand for Dow Chemical, SPCI, Stockholm, 1987

"Le Breakthrough"

1982, Interplas Paris
(Plastics trade fair)

Stand for Dow Chemical Europe S.A.

This stand was designed to present Dow Chemical's new product DOWLEX, an intermediate product in the plastics manufacture, with which Dow Chemical aimed to achieve a breakthrough on the market. Edy Brunner's design for the stand visualized this idea. As the exhibition was being held in France, he and the Dow Chemical staff came up with the motto "Le Breakthrough".

On a trip to the USA, Brunner had seen buildings created by the New York group of architects SITE for a supermarket chain (see: SITE. Architecture as Art. London: Academy Editions, 1980; du, Zürich, 1/1988 "Die New Yorker Gruppe SITE"). This group had considerable success in the USA in the 70s with their dramatic deconstructivist facades, occasionally bordering on the surreal, for otherwise purely functional buildings. The outer walls of a supermarket in Richmond, Virginia, for example, had been designed by the architects in the form of crumbling walls. At one point, there is a deep crack in the wall and rubble has rolled onto the roof of the building.

Edy Brunner created the DOWLEX "breakthrough" in a similar way. The top of one wall of a dark container was pierced and torn open so that the granulate flowed onto the ground in front of it. In front of the half-empty container, a cone-shaped heap partly buried the product information panels. The interior design of the stand was based on Brunner's existing flexible exhibition system, used here on a large scale for the first time. The information panels took the form of flat rectangular boxes filled with the granulate, and with information printed on the plexiglas lids. Neon tubes around the inner edge of the boxes illuminated the product and the texts from the inside.

The give-away was designed by Edy Brunner in the form of the stand: a black cardboard box containing food bags made out of DOWLEX. The box could be torn open in the same way as the container.

Standard Exhibition System for Siemens-Albis AG

1983

In their quest to project a new image at trade fairs, Siemens-Albis commissioned Edy Brunner to design an exhibition system which would be versatile in use and highly efficient in terms of storage. Edy Brunner met these specifications with a modular system of aluminium parts developed on the basis on the experience he had gained in creating his own exhibition system. It is still in use today. The system consists of three basic components: supports, ceiling elements and wall panels. Brunner also designed matching presentation tables for the exhibits.

The rectangular supports are made up of four slim metal components designed for stand heights of 2.5 and 3 m. Metal triangles stabilize the joints with the superimposed ceiling elements. All the loadbearing ceiling beams are made up of 2 m long triangular components which are open to the top. Four of these can be linked to span as much as 8 m without a supporting column. To ensure that these components can be securely linked, Brunner developed a plug-in connection based on his own exhibition system, in this case two conical shells through which an adapter piece is inserted and tightened so that the components remain firmly in place. The ends of the corner elements are bevelled at an angle of 45° to create an elegant finish to the outside of the stand. 4 m long aluminium strips are suspended in the finished structure to create a ceiling in which the lighting system is integrated.

Walls are formed using sandwich panels coated on both sides with Forex. The panels have grooves running along the edges so that they can be linked with interim elements in a variety of materials such as plexiglas, mirror, plastic etc. to create partition walls or completely new rooms. There are also door elements and curved components to create arched or vaulted wall designs. In order to be able to erect the stands direct on the floor of the trade fair hall, Brunner has tucked away all the electrical cabling inside the triangular beams of the ceiling structure. This means there is no need for a raised floor with cables below and also allows the power points to be positioned as required.

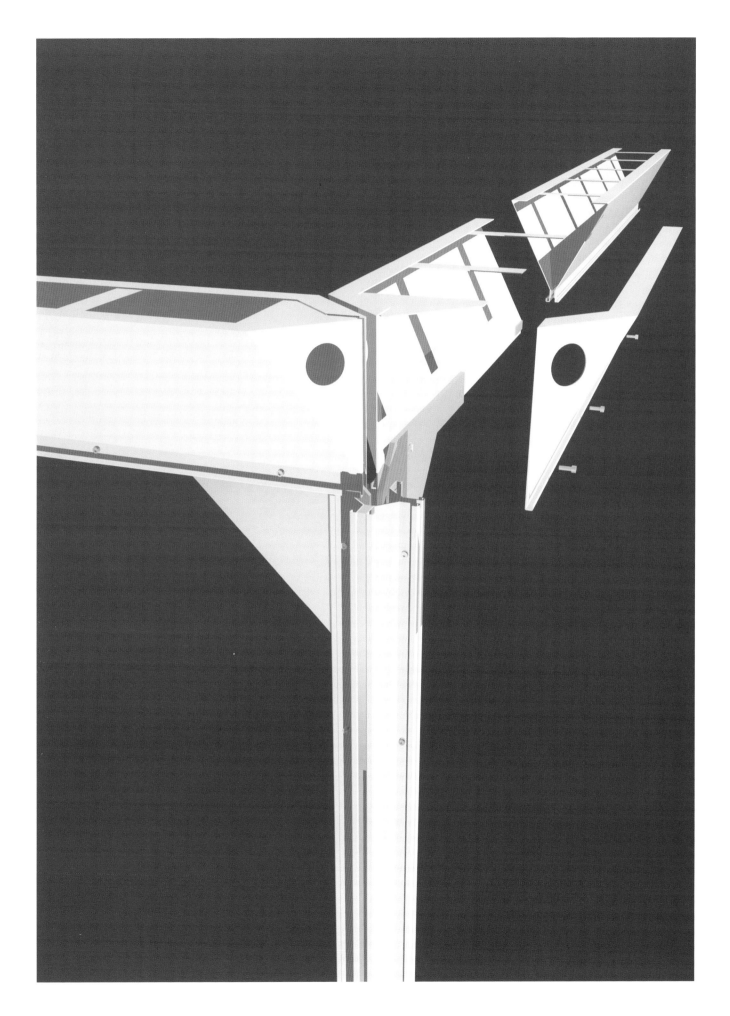

Punk Stand

1983, K '83, Düsseldorf
(International trade fair for plastics and rubber)

Stand for Dow Chemicals Europe S.A.

This may well be regarded as Edy Brunner's most off-beat stand, and it is certainly to the credit of the client Dow Chemical that they allowed the designer so much free rein. Punk had only just arrived from England, and was certainly still far from becoming acceptable in any bourgeois sense of the word, when Brunner took it as his inspiration for the design of this stand. For him, this new trend certainly expressed the spirit of the times. The intended effect was to create a considerable impact with a relatively small stand and allowing the exhibitor to project an image of being "ahead of the times".

The stand consisted of a black cube open at one corner, made of plastic bonded composite boards assembled on a steel structure. With this simple design, Brunner created an area that stood out from the other stands at the fair. Together with the jewellery designer Bernhard Schobinger, and inspired by Schobinger's jewellery, he developed the idea of huge fragments and splinters jutting out of the stand. Schobinger's jewellery combines everyday materials such as fragments of glass, plastic etc. with precious metals.

As Edy Brunner is never content merely to design the architecture of a stand, but invariably seeks to project the overall image of his client at a trade fair, he developed an entire PR-concept in this case, involving an exhibition of Schobinger's jewellery, an accompanying catalogue as a give-away and a press conference. The press response exceeded all expectations.

Bernhard Schobinger's jewellery was presented on plaster casts of naked female busts and arms. On the showcases (as in the catalogue) the materials used were specified, such as "PVC, SHAMPOO, SILVER" or "PLATINUM, POLYETHYLENE, POLYSTYRENE". The message that "all materials, used in the right way, are valuable" was projected in an unconventional way and attracted considerable interest amongst the visitors.

Literature:

DOW DREIUNDACHTZIG. (Exhibition catalogue). Horgen: Dow Chemical Europe, 1983

Granite Stand

1986, K '86, Düsseldorf
(International trade fair for plastics and rubbers)

Stand for Dow Chemical Europe S.A.

Since the 80s, Edy Brunner's exhibition stands have increasingly featured architectural principles. This development reflects his fundamental wish to stand apart from other exhibitors, eschewing fashion trends and swimming agains the tide. The use of unusual materials for temporary exhibition architecture is also in this spirit.

In designing his stands, Edy Brunner invariably seeks to create a clear architectural situation (in other words, creating an impact with open spaces and uncluttered lines rather than with garishness), simple technical structural principles, a self-contained interior. Following the principle of a hall-within-a-hall, he planned this stand in the form of a granite cube with a relatively small entrance at the front. This "foreign body" amongst the other trade fair stands attracted the attention of the public, making visitors curious to see what was on the inside.

The interior, sparse to the point of asceticism (supporting steel structures and granite slabs were visible and not hidden by any superfluous detail) drew the attention of the visitors to the products exhibited. These ranged from shoe soles to CDs to window frames and were presented on slightly inclined metal slabs, turned towards the light. By isolating this exhibition from the rest of the fair, Brunner could ensure that the visitors to the stand were not distracted in any way and were thus the guests of one exhibitor alone.

The idea of using granite was inspired by the immediate surroundings of Brunner's home in Ticino. What is more, granite actually proved to be a relatively economical and robust material. The exhibitor's obligatory give-away, a stone cube citing the form of the stand, was also made of Ticino granite. Brunner took the idea one step further in linking the stand with his own environment. A pillar situated on the exhibition area meant that the stand was actually slightly smaller than the exhibition area available, so he filled the remaining gap around the stand with stone from the area where the trade fair was being held: Thyssen iron ore slag. Brunner repeated this concept in 1987 in Birmingham and in 1988 in Munich, where the stand was used again by Dow Chemical Europe because of the enormous positive feedback it generated amongst visitors.

Edy Brunner's sensitivity in handling materials is also evident in other details. For example, he bevelled the edges of the granite slabs at the corners of the stand so that there were no sharp angles, breaking them so that the thickness of the slabs could no longer be seen. Behind the actual stand, a corrugated metal extension accommodated conference rooms and a small kitchen. To alleviate the harsh contrast between such vastly different materials as granite and corrugated metal, Brunner docked the two elements together with a small intermediate component of hard rubber.

Literature:

Walter Stampa: Edy Brunner, Künstler und Gestalter. In: EXPODATA, Zürich, 4 (April)/1992, p. 24 ff.

Granite stand at Bau 88 in Munich with modified entrance

Granite stand at the Interplas 1987 in Birmingham

Granite stand at the K '86 plastics fair in Düsseldorf

Pages 146/147
Granite stand at the K '86 plastics fair in Düsseldorf

Stand for Dow Chemical Europe S.A.

1988, UTECH '88, The Hague
(Polyurethane conference with exhibition)

In conjunction with a congress on the manufacture and processing of polyurethane foams in The Hague in 1988, an industrial exhibition was held to present the work of companies operating in this field. Rather than simply showing certain individual products, the exhibition aimed to provide information on the companies themselves and their product range in the field of polyurethane production and processing. Accordingly, importance was placed not only the design of the exhibition, but also on the way the overall image of the company exhibiting was projected. The stand was also the venue for the company's PR activities and has to be regarded with this in mind.

The emphasis being on polyurethane, Edy Brunner showed the wide range of uses for this material in daily life, by inviting famous personalities from a variety of fields to have themselves photographed against a neutral background with a plastic cube of polyurethane. The concept was realized by Swiss photographer Christian Vogt who made portraits of Uwe Bahnsen (design), Maria Walliser (sport), Achille Castiglioni (furniture/design), Hans-Joachim Struck (automobile construction), Evelyn Ashford (sport), Max Bill (architecture) and Paul Bocuse (cuisine). The photos were used for a calendar presented by Dow Chemical as a give-away.

Brunner more or less designed the exhibition stand around the photos, which were used as a means of conveying corporate identity. On the rectangular floor area, he placed a semicircular wall dividing the stand two. The apparent volume of the wall created a sense of stability and sold mass, but it was actually supported by the structure of the installation behind it. Behind the wall was a small meeting area and a small kitchen. Opposite the wall, Brunner installed a round bar flanked by a semicircular wall, thereby creating a sense of intimacy for meetings and discussions on the fringe of the conference. The only objects on the large wall were the original photographs by Christian Vogt with their brief accompanying texts – as this was a specialist conference, no detailed explanations were required. In this way, Brunner created a stand that had little in common with a purely industrial exhibition space. Instead, with its bar, it was an attractive meeting place.

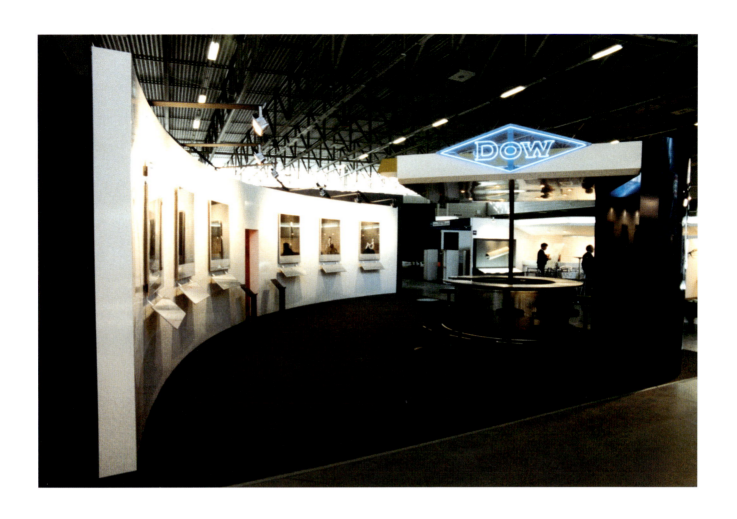

Page 151: Edy Brunner's calendar with photos by
Christian Vogt, designed as a promotional gift.
From top left to bottom right:
Maria Walliser, Achille Castiglioni, Hans-Joachim Stuck,
Evelyn Ashford, Max Bill, Paul Bocuse.

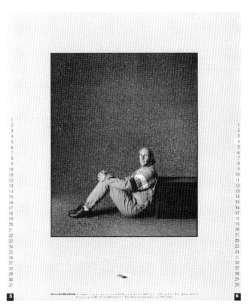

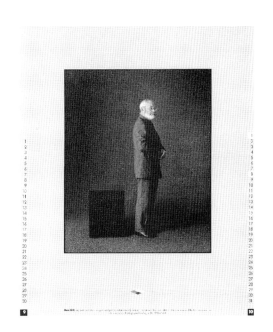

Masonry Stand

1989, K '89, Düsseldorf
(International trade fair for plastic and rubber)

Stand for Dow Chemical Europe S.A.

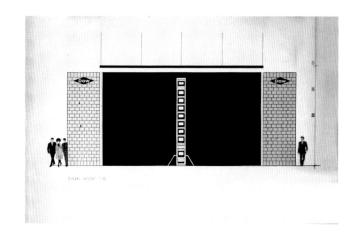

As with his 1986 Granite Stand, Edy Brunner employed unusual materials to create yet another remarkable stand for Dow Chemical at the 1989 plastics trade fair in Düsseldorf. This time, he built a stand of exposed concrete, contrasting and corresponding with the steel and corrugated metal used on the inside. This material also has distinct advantages. It is cheap, strong, fireproof and recyclable. Again, Brunner was counting on the impact of the unexpected: stone at a plastics trade fair.

The increasing emphasis on architectural elements in Brunner's work in the 80s is particularly evident here. He went beyond the bounds of conventional temporary stand design by creating a two-storey architectural structure of traditional building materials, based on the fundamental principles of structural engineering, and eschewing all aspirations to faddish trends. In the meantime, Brunner had come to the conclusion that well-founded, quality design had become something to be taken for granted and was therefore no longer anything special, but merely the basic precondition for all activities in this field.

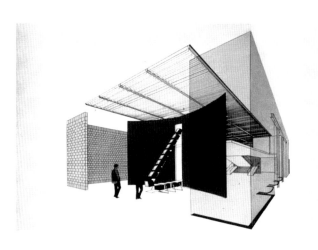

Once again, the design was based on the principle of a hall-within-a-hall. The greater the hustle and bustle at the industrial trade fairs, the more Brunner began closing his stands to allow visitors to concentrate more fully on the information and products offered by the exhibitors. What is more, he created an area for business meetings on the open upper level. In order to achieve maximum use of the available space, Brunner designed this stand, for the first time, to have a floor space corresponding precisely with the demarcation line of the designated exhibition area. He was assisted in the architectural design by the firm of architects M. Geisser / H. Gies.

Information for the public was screened on TV monitors in the form of video clips. Taking up this concept, Edy Brunner created a "video conveyor" for the stand based on the idea of the "Apple Music Box" video environments he had designed together with Francesco Mariotti. In collaboration with a leading manufacturer of conveyor systems (primarily for the printing industry) a conveyor belt was created on which the TV monitors moved, showing video clips of information by the exhibitor. Flanked by two corrugated metal walls, the "video conveyor belt" was the focal point of the stand.

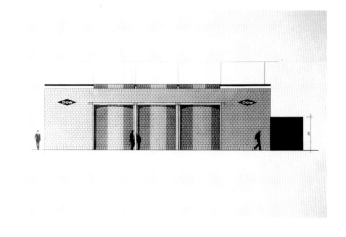

From top to bottom:
Front of stand with video conveyor belt
Overall view
Side view of stand

Corrugated Metal Stand

1989, DEUBAU 89, Essen
(Construction materials trade fair)

Stand for Dow Deutschland Inc.

Like the stand at the 1982 Interplas in Paris, this stand was intended solely as a means of presenting a single product by Dow Chemical. FLOORMATE was a new and highly resilient flooring isolation material. In designing the stand (and the overall image of the company at the exhibition) Edy Brunner sought to visualize this feature clearly. For this purpose, he created an extremely robust table with a steel worktop. On each of the four corners of the worktop, he placed one FLOOR-MATE tile (25 x 25 cm) with a sheet of Plexiglas in the same size above and below. On this, he placed a 5 tonne stone. This demonstration of the resilience of FLOORMATE (20 t/m^2 was so striking that the installation drew considerable attention at the exhibition and became a real crowd-puller.

The installation with the stone was placed at the outer border of the stand area to act as an eye-catcher. The stand itself consisted of three different corrugated metal spaces. Display panels were hung on a curved wall. Adjacent to this was a small bar with a round floor area closed off to the rear by a semicircular corrugated metal wall. A closed-off, elliptically shaped section for technical services was adjoined. This was the first time Brunner had created a stand entirely of corrugated metal. The homogeneity of the material used permitted him to create a wide range of different open and closed forms on a relatively small space while avoiding any sense of clutter.

Roofscape

1990, Constructa, Hanover
(Construction materials trade fair)

Stand for Dow Deutschland Inc.

There are two basic requirements of an exhibition stand which, at first glance, would appear to be mutually exclusive: transparency and maximum public attraction on the one hand and relative seclusion from the trade fair on the other hand. Externally attractive closed stands such as the "Punk Stand", the "Granite Stand" and the "Masonry Stand" are one possibile solution to the problem. Another is the approach developed by Edy Brunner with astonishing ease and simplicity for the stand at the Constructa fair.

Two large, tilted corrugated metal walls facing each other were the dominant design features, reducing the stand to a passageway open at both ends and creating the impression of a roof-top situation. The strictly symmetrical arrangement of the few objects present (counter, visitors' table, trees) were emphasized by the design intention of dispensing with all ornamental additions and limiting the technical execution to structural necessities alone.

One of the walls had an opening (created by omitting two wall segments in the central axis) leading to a meeting room with bar and adjacent technical service areas. Brunner created this tract using his own versatile exhibition system. The stand was roofed by a textile ceiling spotlit from below so that the entire room was bathed in an even light.

Swiss Pavilion

1991, Telecom 91, Geneva
(International telecommunications exhibition)

Unlike previous exhibition stands designed by Edy Brunner, this pavilion was not intended as an individual stand for the presentation of a single company at an industrial exhibition. In this case, a more generous setting had to be created to accommodate the stands of several different exhibitors. Edy Brunner contrasted the variety of different forms of trade fair buildings at industrial exhibitions with a simple hall-within-a-hall. It had to offer all the typical functions and facilities of a trade fair hall on the inside, while projecting an aesthetically attractive appearance and effective advertising message on the outside. This was his greatest challenge so far, as it went far beyond the requirements of individual trade fair construction. In fact, it began where most trade fair design projects end. His considerable experience in the field of trade fair design proved to be a great advantage in finding a solution to this particular problem. Structural calculations were made by engineer Peter Osterwalder and Edy Brunner also had the support and assistance of the firm of architects M. Geisser / H. Gies, with whom he had already collaborated on other projects.

In order to make the best possible use of the overall available space, he created a pavilion that would cover the precise area designated. This gave him a rectangular floor area which he then divided up into a grid of 40 (8 x 5) squares of equal size (7 x 7 m). The simplest structural form to use was a box, which could be easily built using a modular steel system. Taking the grid division of the floor plan as his basis, Brunner developed the structural principle of the hall on the basis of 7 x 7 m boxes with a height of 4 m. Apart from the loadbearing pillars required at the edges of each box, this resulted in a spacious interior space providing the 28 individual exhibitors the greatest possible freedom to design their own stands. Brunner made no attempt to hide the steel structure behind any additional decorative elements, integrating it instead in the overall aesthetic system of the structure. The transparency of the building as a whole was achieved by using glass slats instead of closed walls. This created the impression that the pavilion could be seen from the side as an optically closed building, while the front view provided a maximum insight into the interior. What is more, the lighting of the white glass strips created the optical impression of a "body of light", giving the steel structure additional elegance and lightness.

At the intersections of the corridors, Edy Brunner opened up the corners of the pavilion to provide access from both sides. A central courtyard created an appealing focal point which attracted visitors. From here, all the stands on the first floor and the restaurant on the second floor were easily acces-

Model

sible via a spacious stairway or a hydraulically operated glass elevator affording views of the entire courtyard. As the restaurant on the second floor did not cover the entire floor area, it looked as though it had been dropped on top of the pavilion. From here, there were views of the "stand landscape" of the entire trade fair hall.

Literature:

TELECOM 91. Weltschau der Telekommunikation. In: Rivista delle PTT, Bern, 11/1991, p. 14 f.

Walter Stampa: Edy Brunner, Künstler und Gestalter. In: EXPODATA, Zürich, 4 (April)/1992, p. 24 ff.

Stand for Dow Deutschland, Inc.

1992, Constructa, Hanover
(Construction materials trade fair)

Edy Brunner's aim of reducing an exhibition stand to its bare structural necessities while working to the highest standards of perfection using state of the art technology (e.g. computer-aided production of iron components) is reflected most clearly in his stand for the 1992 Constructa.

The basic motif of this stand is, once again, that of a passageway or corridor situation, echoing the slanted walls of the stand built for the 1990 Constructa. Taking up the challenge of presenting realistic models on a scale of 1:1 to demonstrate the various uses of insulating materials for flat roofs, Brunner developed a loadbearing system for these large, heavy models (2,4 m x 3,6 m) made of triangular 6 m high steel components. Six models were displayed, each of them installed between two such loadbearing steel components. The loadbearing components were designed to fulfil their structural functions as simply as possible (supporting the 1:1 scale models, holding the ceiling fabric and lighting, carrying individual spotlights).

The twelve steel components defined the overall area of the stand. As the (triangular) interior rooms of the components were closed with grey injection moulded plastic compound slabs and the slanted wall leaned into the stand, the impression created was similar to that of the stand at the 1990 Constructa. Nevertheless, the triangular structural elements had the appearance of a row of slats creating a closed plane when viewed from the side, though the overall view was one of spacious clarity, thus lending the structure a sense of lightness that was further enhanced by the design details.

Forex Stand

1992, K '92, Düsseldorf
(International plastics and rubber trade fair)

Stand for Alusuisse-Lonza Holding AG

Alusuisse-Lonza AG is a group of companies with a broad product range which has undergone sweeping changes in recent years. It presented its new corporate identity for the first time at the K '92. For this trade fair visit, a prestigious and spacious stand was to be created on a relatively small exhibition area, with the focus entirely on corporate image rather than product presentation.

Edy Brunner concentrated on two fundamental ideas. As a basic design motif, he chose the diagonal, dividing the stand into two sections with three 6 m high structures and lending it the monumentality and spaciousness requested by the exhibitor. The floor of the stand, all the fittings and furnishings as well as other important details were made of Forex, which is an A-L product.

The diagonal wall of large Forex components divided the stand into two distinct areas. The larger front area served to provide general information on the company and for initial business contacts. At the front right hand corner, there was a round information counter whose perforated outer wall was lined with red Forex to create a coloured accent in the white and brightly lit exhibition area. For the stand, Edy Brunner created a sculpture made of two interconnected pieces of black and white Forex hung from the hall ceiling and floating over the information counter. This sculpture was produced as a multiple and given away to visitors.

The walls to the rear of the stand were mirror-clad to make the room look bigger. The bar was situated here, as well as an area with tubular steel chairs and round tables for customer discussions, and also a kitchen or storeroom.

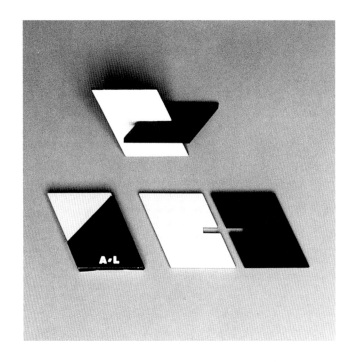

Top:
Multiple as give-away art.
The design was based on the A-L logo, with the shape of the interlocking elements in aluminium and Forex (plastic) derived from the hyphen in order to visualize the company's aluminium and plastics production. Variations were made using different coloured Forex.

Bottom:
Large-scale sculptural object of interlocking Forex elements at the opening of the Edy Brunner exhibition at the Alusuisse-Lonza AG headquarters in Zürich.
The sculpture was first shown in 1992, suspended above the "Forex Stand".

174

Stand for Schindler Lifts Ltd

1993, Swissbau 93, Basel
(Construction exhibition)

The theme of this stand was the technical backfitting of elevators in buildings. The aim was to present the various possibilities available. As an eye-catcher, a fully functional elevator was installed in front of the facade of a trompe l'oeil historic facade. Visitors could take the elevator up from the lower floor of the stand where the reception counter and an exhibition of elevator shafts were situated.

From the upper exit of the elevator, a metal bridge led to the upper level of the stand on the first floor of the exhibition hall. This upper level housed the service facilities and public area, the meeting rooms and cafeteria. In order to create a monumental and spacious effect, Brunner positioned the most important feature of the stand, the elevator with the metal bridge, at an angle across the corner of the stand so that it could be seen from several sides.

He created a ceiling of spanned white textile, spotlit so that the overall area could be seen. The rear wall of the upper floor was closed by a simple steel frame structure with corrugated metal walls.

Stand for Schindler Lifts Ltd and C.O.A.M. SpA

Interlift 94, Augsburg
(International trade fair for elevator technology)

As the overall theme in this case was the presentation of components for the manufacture of elevators, part of the stand was allocated to the Schindler's Italian subsidiary C.O.A.M. SpA, a manufacturer of hydraulic aggregates. In other words, two distinctly separate areas had to be created within the same stand to ensure that each exhibitor had their own area. Moreover, a wide variety of exhibits had to be presented in a way that was both clear and informative.

Edy Brunner chose as his key design motif a curved wall made of a steel frame filled with wire mesh in the form of an industrial storage shelf. This structure acted as a partition dividing the stand two separate areas while still allowing visitors on either side to see the other exhibitor. In order to make the best possible use of the relatively small exhibition area, he placed this wall diagonally across the stand area which is delineated only by the floor covering (placed directly on the floor of the hall) and the white sailcloth spotlit from below.

The wall opens up onto a larger, sparsely furnished area. In the corner opposite the wall, there is a round reception counter whose reduced technoid form (a steel framework clad in perforated metal) corresponds to the curved wall, and visually closes the stand. One third of the wall, to the left, is given over to a number of metal tables with tubular steel chairs for contact discussions, while the rest of the area is earmarked for the presentation of exhibits. The wall also serves as a presentation area, with individual exhibits displayed on its shelves, some of them still on wooden pallets just as they might be seen in some large industrial warehouse or delivered direct to the customer. What is more, the technical facilities, storeroom and kitchen were also integrated into the wall, with a connecting doorway to the exhibition area on the other side.

The smaller stand area behind the wall was used by the second exhibitor, C.O.A.M. SpA. It was also designed to accommodate customer talks. Here, too, there was a circular reception counter and some tables and chairs. As an eye-catcher at the corner of the stand, there was a "ball track" specially developed for this trade fair; a spiral structure on which a ball rolled downwards and, on arriving at the bottom, was raised again by a hydraulic lift produced by C.O.A.M. and then allowed to roll back down again. This was a visually appealing way of presenting the exhibitor's product functionally without having to go into theoretical explanations of the technical details.

Stand for Schindler Lifts Ltd

Swissbau 95, Basel
(Construction trade fair)

The prime purpose of this stand was to present the new "Schindler 300". Prefabricated concrete shaft components for new buildings or for backfitting elevators in existing buildings were to be shown here. The exhibition area was the same as at Swissbau 93. Again, the stand was built on two levels, with access to the upper level by elevator.

The freestanding elevator column clad in prefabricated concrete components acted as an eye-catcher. To make the best possible use of the available space, Brunner designed the elevator shaft on a diagonal, further emphasized by the fact that the metal floor and metal grid of the bridge did not simply end at the upper floor, but were continued to create a visually uniform corridor crossing the entire stand.

The ground floor of the stand served as a reception and exhibition area. The elevator to the upper level could be entered from a raised platform. From the upper exit of the elevator, the visitor could reach all the other facilities of the stand. Computer simulations were screened on monitors showing various different functions of elevators. The meeting area and the cafeteria were aligned along the corridor.

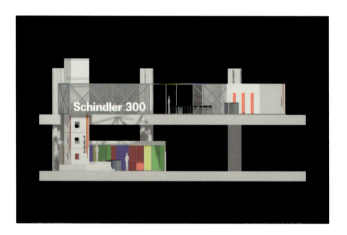

Stand for Dow Deutschland, Inc.

1995, Bau 95, Munich
(Construction trade fair)

As there were plans for this stand to be used at the major German construction trade fairs in Munich, Hanover and Berlin with their different respectively exhibition areas, considerable flexibility was called for in adapting the size of the stand without allowing it to lose its distinctive character.

In keeping with his designs for previous construction exhibition stands, Brunner chose to use individual metal components rather than a self-contained architectural approach to define the stand area while structuring the 1:1 models of building materials and insulation materials displayed between them.

In addition to the models, information panels with integrated monitors were also installed. These could be viewed from the outside, creating the situation of a market stall on which products are presented towards the outside. For those interested in further information, consultancy was available inside the stand.

The wing-like structure of the large components served as an eye-catcher for the public. Each component actually consisted of two aluminium sheet wings joined on a curved axis. A sweeping horizontal wing spanning 10 m "floated" at a height of 5.5 m, held in position only by a steel wire fixed at the short end, and anchored to the base of the vertical wing.

On the opposite side, the stand was closed off by a slightly curved wall of dark grey sheet metal, behind which further areas such as the meeting area, kitchen and storeroom were accommodated. A bar was placed in front of the wall. In the middle of the stand there was a round information desk.

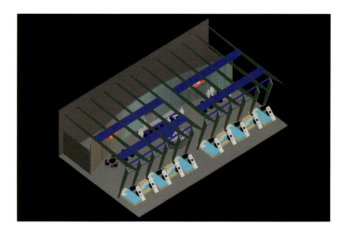

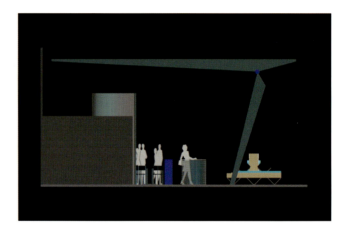

Outlook

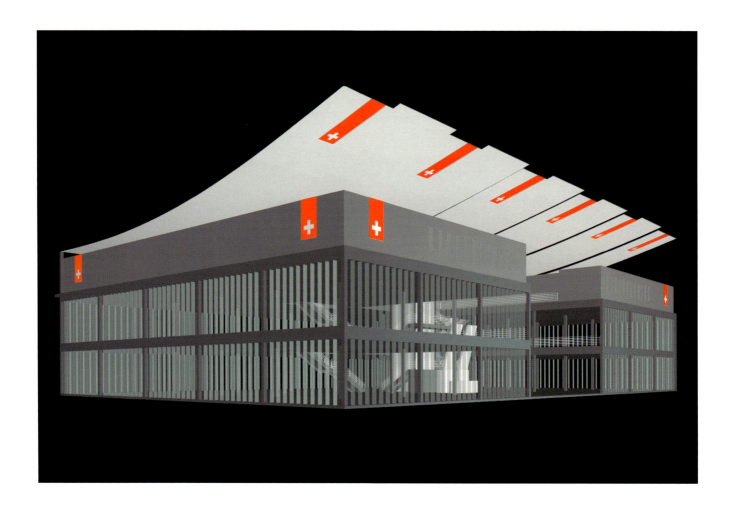

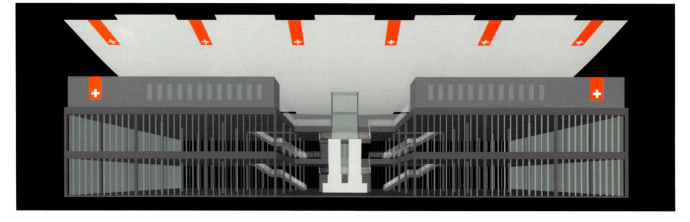

Swiss Pavilion
Telecom 95, Geneva

The modular steel construction system used for the Swiss
Pavilion at Telecom 91 was used here in a modified form. Edy
Brunner designed a restructured pavilion on the same floor
area. The courtyard of the new pavilion now opens out
towards the main flow of visitors. The "video conveyor belt"
developed in 1989 adds an additional focal point. The full floor
area of the upper level can now be used. A roof spans the
entire pavilion, and is an eye-catcher even at a distance.

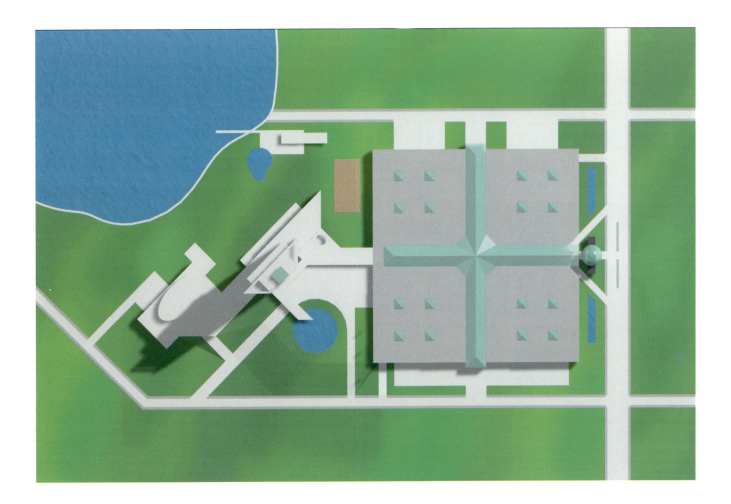

Project for an exhibition area in Hanoi, Vietnam
In collaboration with raumtechnik Messebau GmbH
(a member of the Daimler-Benz Interservices group)

Because of his practical experience in the field of trade fairs and
exhibitions, Edy Brunner was invited by the raumtechnik
company to draw up a concept for the entire complex. His considerable expertise allowed him to develop a project on this
scale with a view to smooth operation and efficiency. In for-
mulating his plans, he collaborated with the designer Walter
Leuthold. The area consists of four interlinked exhibition halls
with a main entrance in the form of a large glass sphere.

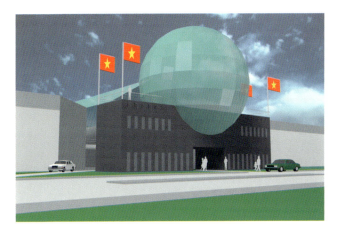

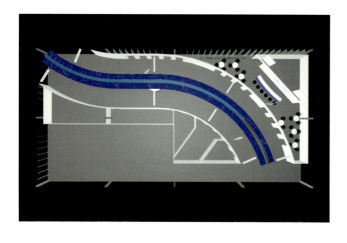

Stand for Landis & Gyr
Telecom 95, Geneva

Stand designed in the form of a meandering walled passageway within which the exhibits are shown as a "strip of stars" ceiling structure. The area outside the passageway holds a cafeteria, meeting areas, kitchen and storeroom.

Stand for Graf + Cie. AG
ITMA 95, Milan

In order to project a technological atmosphere, Brunner designed the stand in raw steel. Stringent restrictions imposed by the trade fair organizers obliged him to reduce the architecture considerably. The focal point of the design is the central axis. Brunner's design deliberately ignored the five pillars of the trade fair hall on the area of the stand, making them appear as distinct intrusions. The stand is open to attract visitors and the company's exhibits, displayed in four illuminated showcases, can be seen from both sides

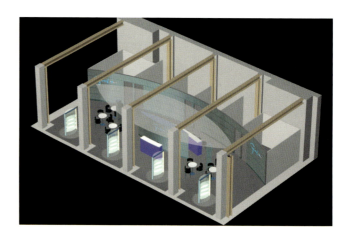

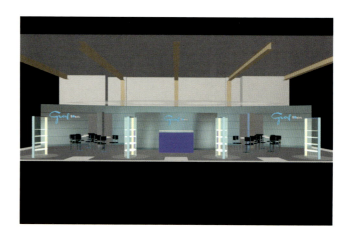

"Dresden in Hamburg"
Exhibition with large format copies of panorama photographs from the Dresden series

In 1994, Edy Brunner spent three months in Hamburg. Being in touch with interested insiders meant that he was able to follow up an idea he had been nurturing since his exhibition in Dresden the previous year. Since the unification of Germany, there has been a lively cultural exchange between Hamburg and Dresden. Having created his panorama photographs in Dresden during a period of political upheaval and having exhibited them there shortly afterwards, Brunner had soon begun to toy with the idea of showing his Dresden photographs in Hamburg in order to create an exhibition of a city in the city: "Dresden in Hamburg". The concept of the exhibition is to create large format copies of the Dresden panorama photographs and display them on billboards throughout Hamburg. In this way, the entire city of Hamburg would become a gallery. The exhibition would be commented in detail in at least one Hamburg daily newspaper. A streetplan would pinpoint the locations of the large format copies and all the photographs would be shown. Edy Brunner has already examined the technical and organizational aspects of implementing this project together with a poster corporation and a specialist photo lab in Hamburg. The exhibition can go ahead with the official support of the twin cities of Dresden and Hamburg.

Resümee

Ein Feuerwerk von Ideen und Konzepten und eine Fülle von künstlerischen und gestalterischen Realisationen – wie beschreibt man einen Künstler, dessen gestalterisches Spektrum von Concept Art über kinetische Kunst, serielle Kunst, Environment, Umgebungsgestaltung und Kunst für den öffentlichen Raum, Innenarchitektur und Ausstellungsgestaltung bis hin zur Fotografie reicht? Dem Künstler Edy Brunner mit einer Klassifizierung gerecht werden zu wollen, hieße, seine künstlerische Intention bereits im Ansatz mißzuverstehen. Denn worum geht es einem Mann, dessen Kreativität ihn auf verschiedenste Schaffensgebiete zwingt, auf deren jedem einzelnen er aufsehenerregende Werke hervorbringt, um sich danach wieder neu zu orientieren und sich völlig anderen Problemstellungen zuzuwenden? Läßt sich mit einem solchen Œuvre ein eigener Stil entwickeln, der nach außen hin ablesbar ist?

In der Tat sind es zuerst Fragen, die angesichts des Schaffens des Vielseitigen auftreten. Das Werk des 1943 geborenen Berners bietet eines nicht: vorgefertigte, leicht konsumierbare Antworten. Mit seinen Arbeiten verführt uns der Künstler dazu, seinem konzeptuellen Ansatz zu folgen und selbst geistig kreativ zu werden. Meist findet er in seiner unmittelbaren Umgebung Situationen vor, an denen er überraschende geistige Zusammenhänge entdeckt, die in ihm ein assoziatives Gedankenspiel auslösen, das schließlich zur Visualisierung einer bestimmten Grundidee führt. Dabei ist ihm die adäquate Umsetzung des so gewonnenen Konzeptes wichtiger als das Medium, mit dessen Hilfe dies geschieht. Er wählt sich immer das Passende.

Edy Brunner ist seit 30 Jahren künstlerisch tätig. Eine eingehende künstlerische Ausbildung, etwa in Form eines Akademiestudiums, hat er nie genossen. In diesem Sinne ist er ein Autodidakt. Das garantiert ihm bis heute den unkonventionellen Umgang mit künstlerischen Medien. Was Brunner immer schon ausgezeichnet hat, ist das schnelle Erfassen auch komplizierter Situationen und Zusammenhänge. Willy Rotzler nennt dies seine «Gabe zu sehen». Sie ist Brunners besonderes Talent und Grundlage jeder seiner kreativen Äußerungen. Ob er Alltagsgegenstände, wie Steckdosen, Schrauben oder Kunstblumen zu Objekten mit hintergründig witziger Aussage verarbeitet, ob er Prozesse in fotografische Einzelbilder zerlegt und so, auf große Tableaus montiert, dokumentiert, ob er aus riesigen Findlingen den Vorplatz einer großen Versicherungsgesellschaft mit einer kinetischen Brunnenanlage gestaltet, den Messestand eines Kunststoffherstellers in Form eines großen Würfels aus Granit projektiert oder Stadtlandschaften mit einer Panoramakamera dokumentiert, immer steht dahinter ein schlüssiges Konzept, das Momente des Alltäglichen – Situationen, Prozesse, Gegenstände und Materialien – im Licht ästhetischer Gesetzmäßigkeit erscheinen läßt.

Anhand der wichtigsten Arbeiten von Edy Brunner soll hier seine gestalterische Intention deutlich gemacht werden. Da er selbst definitive, fertige Zustände ablehnt, kann auch dieses Buch kein fertiges Bild des Ruhelosen zeichnen. Schon die Gliederung in die Kapitel Konzept und Kunst, Fotografie und Design ist eine Einschränkung der Sicht, da Brunner vieles parallel geschaffen hat. Aber auf diese Weise werden Schritte und Brüche seiner Entwicklung sichtbar und nachvollziehbar. In vielen Facetten wird Brunners Auseinandersetzung mit seiner Umwelt spürbar: kritisch, aber nicht mit erhobenem Zeigefinger. Daß er sich nicht auf ein «Markenzeichen» festlegen läßt, macht ihn dem Kunstmarkt verdächtig, untermauert aber die Glaubwürdigkeit dessen, was er uns mitteilt.

Axel Wendelberger
Zürich, April 1995

Résumé

Un feu d'artifice d'idées et de concepts, une œuvre multiple et multiforme – comment décrire un artiste, dont le champ d'activités va de l'art conceptuel à la photographie, en passant par l'art cinétique et sériel, l'aménagement de l'espace environnant de manière à transformer le spectateur en acteur, l'art des espaces publics, l'architecture d'intérieur et l'aménagement d'expositions? Tenter de classer Edy Brunner dans une quelconque catégorie équivaudrait à passer à côté de son approche même de la création. Quelles sont les motivations d'un homme, dont la créativité déborde sur les champs artistiques les plus divers, lui permettant chacun de créer des œuvres hors du commun, et de rebondir ensuite pour se consacrer à des problématiques tout autres? Un style propre, compréhensible pour le public peut-il se dégager d'une telle création?

En effet, l'œuvre de cet artiste aux multiples talents suscite nombre de questions. Une chose est certaine: le Bernois né en 1943 offre tout sauf des réponses toutes faites et facilement «consommables». Par ses œuvres, Edy Brunner nous invite à le suivre sur la voie conceptuelle pour devenir créateurs à notre tour. Souvent, son environnement le plus proche lui fait découvrir des corrélations surprenantes, déclenchant un processus associatif qui conduit finalement à la visualisation d'une idée de base. Par la suite, la traduction adéquate de ce concept dans la réalité devient prioritaire par rapport au support choisi. Support qui, néanmoins, se révèle toujours particulièrement adapté.

Edy Brunner se consacre à la création depuis 30 ans, sans avoir jamais suivi de formation spécifique, que ce soit sous forme de cours d'académie ou autres. Il mérite ainsi pleinement le qualificatif d'autodidacte qui, jusqu'à ce jour, nous gratifie d'une manière peu conventionnelle de manier les différents instruments de la création artistique. Edy Brunner s'est toujours distingué par sa faculté de saisir rapidement des situations et des corrélations complexes. Willy Rotzler qualifie cette faculté de «don de voir plus loin» – un don qui est à la base de son expression artistique. Qu'il travaille sur des objets quotidiens, comme des prises électriques, des vis ou des fleurs artificielles, pour leur faire transmettre un message drôle. Qu'il décompose des processus complexes pour les reconstituer photographiquement sur de grands tableaux. Qu'il aménage l'entrée d'une grande société d'assurances au moyen de blocs erratiques plantés dans un décor de fontaines cinétiques. Qu'il esquisse le stand d'un fabricant de plastiques à l'image d'un grand dé en granit. Qu'il fasse le portrait d'une ville au moyen de photos panoramiques. Toujours sa démarche, guidée par un concept pertinent, dégage du quotidien – des situations, processus, objets et matériaux – certaines lois esthétiques supérieures.

Ce recueil des œuvres les plus importantes d'Edy Brunner se veut le reflet de son expression et de ses motivations artistiques. Cependant, l'image ainsi crée ne saurait être figée, comme le créateur toujours en mouvement refuse lui-même le définitif. D'ailleurs, à elle seule, la division en chapitres – Concept et Art, Photographie et Design – est réductrice, vu qu'Edy Brunner a crée de nombreuses œuvres en parallèle. Cette manière de procéder permet toutefois de rendre apparentes les différentes étapes et ruptures de son parcours. Son rapport à l'environnement se manifeste de mille façons, l'artiste se montrant critique, mais sans pointer du doigt. Qu'il ne se laisse pas réduire à une «image de marque» le rend suspect sur le marché de l'art, mais ne fait que conforter la crédibilité de son message.

Axel Wendelberger
Zurich, Avril 1995

Sinopsis

Un estallido de ideas, de inventiva, tal profusión de obras de arte y de diseño. ¿cómo describir a un artista cuya obra abarca un espectro tan complejo que va desde el arte conceptual hasta el diseño de exposiciones y la fotografía, atravesando el género cinético, la composición serial, el environment, el diseño de exteriores, las obras de arte en plazas y recintos públicos y la arquitectura de interiores? Cualquier intento por clasificar a Edy Brunner implica interpretar en forma radicalmente equivocada su intencionalidad artística. ¿Qué busca, en definitiva, este hombre, a quien su creatividad impulsa a adentrarse en los más diversos ámbitos del quehacer artístico, produciendo en cada uno de ellos obras sensacionales, para cambiar de rumbo inmediatamente y dedicarse a problemas totalmente diferentes? ¿Es posible desarrollar en una obra de estas características un estilo propio e inteligible para quien la contempla?

Preguntas y más preguntas que surgen inevitablemente frente a la creación de este artista polifacético. Y si hay algo que no ofrece, ciertamente, la obra de este suizo nacido en Berna en 1943 son respuestas prefabricadas de fácil consumo. Con sus realizaciones, el artista nos induce a asumir su enfoque conceptual y a dar rienda suelta a nuestra propio espíritu creador. Con frecuencia tropieza en su entorno inmediato con situaciones en las que descubre las conexiones más sorprendentes, poniendo en marcha un juego de ideas y asociaciones que culmina, finalmente, en la visualización de una idea básica determinada. En este proceso, da más importancia a la materialización precisa de esa idea que al medio del cual se vale para lograrlo. Siempre elige el medio adecuado.

Edy Brunner viene dedicándose al arte desde hace treinta años. No aprendió su oficio en una academia de bellas artes. En este sentido, es un autodidacta. Ello le permite hasta hoy valerse de los medios artísticos sin atender a las convenciones. Brunner se ha caracterizado siempre por captar con celeridad situaciones y nexos causales complejos. Willy Rotzler ha dicho que Brunner posee «el don de ver». Éste es, en efecto, el gran talento de Brunner y la base de cada una de sus expresiones artísticas. Lo mismo toma objetos cotidianos, como enchufes, tornillos o flores artificiales, ensamblándolos en una composición de mensaje sutil y burlón, que descompone un proceso en imágenes fotográficas aisladas para montarlos luego sobre grandes tableaus, construye una fuente cinética con gigantescos bloques erráticos delante de la sede de una importante compañía de seguros, diseña para un fabricante de plásticos un stand cúbico de roca granítica o capta el paisaje urbano con su cámara panorámica: Detrás de todas sus actividades hay, invariablemente, una idea concluyente que pone de relieve lo cotidiano – situaciones, procesos, objetos y materiales – a la luz de los cánones estéticos.

La intención creadora de Edy Brunner debe ser elucidada aquí a través de sus trabajos más importantes. El propio Brunner rechaza la idea de que cualquier estadio pueda sera acabado y definitivo. Tampoco el libro podrá sino dar un boceto tentativo de su inquietud artística. Ya la simple inclusión de las obras en capítulos: Concepción y Arte, Fotografía y Diseño, limita la perspectiva, ya que Brunner ha creado muchas de ellas simultáneamente y en forma paralela. Sin embargo, de este modo se ponen de manifiesto algunas etapas y fisuras de su evolución artística. El enfrentamiento de Brunner con su entorno – crítico, pero nunca admonitorio – es perceptible en muchas facetas. La imposibilidad de encasillarlo en un estilo despierta las suspicacias del mercado de arte. Y a la vez cimenta la credibilidad de lo que nos transmite.

Axel Wendelberger
Zurich, April 1995

概要

爆発するようにほとばしり出てくるアイデア、芸術的創造性のひらめき——この芸術家を説明するのに一体どこから始めたら良いだろうか？　彼の作品は、コンセプトアートからキネテイックアート、またシリアル芸術から環境芸術に至るまで広い範囲にわたる——その中間には環境芸術のためのディザイン、公共空間の芸術、室内装飾、展示ディザイン、そして写真術さえも包みこむ——。エデイ・ブルンナーを分類にあてはめようとするのは、最初の第一歩から彼の芸術上の意図を誤って解釈している。これほどまでに多様な作品に駆り立て、どの分野でも全くセンセーショナルな作品を生みだし、かと思うと次には新しい方向に向かって全く別の課題を取り上げる、そういう創作エネルギーをもつ男の背後にある原動力はどのようなものだろうか？　作品がこのような範囲の広さと多様性を持っているのを考えると、他と判然と区別できるはっきりとした独特の個人的芸術様式をもつというのは可能なのだろうか？

1943年ベルリンで生まれたこの多才な芸術家の作品について考える時、これらの問いが必ず出てくる。彼の作品はどれを見ても、それが簡単に到達しえたものでないことがうかがえる。作品はわれわれを魅了し彼のコンセプトアートの中に巻き込む、われわれ自身の創造的、知的能力を働かせることを求める。エデイー・ブルンナーは、身近な環境の中である驚くべき共時性に照準をあてて、そこから一連の連想を喚起させる。それが極に達した時、ある根本的なアイデアの芸術的具象化となる。ここでは、表現媒体が何であるかよりも、コンセプトにぴったりとしたふさわしい転置であるかどうかの方が彼には重要である。適切であればどんな媒体物でも選択してしまう。

エデイー・ブルンナーは、30年間芸術家として仕事をしている。大学の研究課程という形での特定の訓練を受けたことのない彼は独学の芸術家と言えよう。この事ゆえに、彼の美術表現のための媒体物についてアプローチは全生涯を通じて必ずいつも自由である。ブルンナーは、相対的位置関係や情況がどんなに複雑なものであれ、すぐに全体を見てとることが可能であった。これを「見ることに対する天賦の才」とウイリー・ロツラーは表現する。これはブルンナーの特別な才能であり、彼のすべての独創的表現の源である。日常の事物（ソケット、ねじ、造花など）から神秘的で機知にあふれる作品を創造する時も、過程を一つ一つの写真像に分解して大きなタブロー形式に記録する、あるいは大保険会社の正面玄関に飾るキネテイックアートとしての荒削りの巨大な玉石でつくった噴水、プラスチックメーカーのために国際見本市に展示するスタンドを花崗岩の大きな方体でディザインする時も、またパノラマカメラで都会の景色を撮る時も、すべて背後には入念に考えつくされたコンセプトが存在している。美学的に計算された光の下に、日常生活の様相——たとえば、建物などの位置、場所、変化、事物、材料など——が姿を現わす。

本論文は、エデイー・ブルンナーの最も優れた作品を通して、彼の創作意図を説明しようとするものである。限定的で窮極的なものを彼自身が拒否しているように、この精力的な芸術家についてここで述べるにあたって何も結論的なことをいうことはできない。コンセプト及び芸術、写真術、ディザインという章に分けること自体、われわれの洞察をさえぎるものとなる——というのは、ブルンナーは数多くの作品を同時並例的に創作していたからだ。しかし、章に分けることで彼の進歩発達の段階や変化を明らかにすることができる。環境に対する彼のアプローチ——批評的ではあるがごうまんではない——がいろいろとはっきり見えてくる。ブルンナーは、作品には一度も自分のいわゆる「認刻極印」を用いたことがない。この事は、美術品市場では彼を疑わしく感じさせている。しかし反面、彼がわれわれに伝えようとしているメッセージの真実性を強く感じさせる。

アツェット・ウエンデルバーガー
1995年4月　チューリッヒ

Appendix

Biographical notes

Edy Brunner was born on 19 October 1943 in Bern where he went to school and later completed an apprenticeship in photographic retouching.

From 1964 to 1966, Brunner was employed as a graphic artist at the legendary advertising agency GGK (Gerstner, Gredinger, Kutter) in Basel. In the early 60s, it was one of the largest and most innovative agencies in Switzerland, renowned for the intelligence and creativity of its approach. The stimulating atmosphere there made a deep impression on Edy Brunner. Karl Gerstner, in particular, who later left the field of advertising to devote himself entirely to art, encouraged him to address questions of constructive and serial art. Soon he began to experiment with photograms, on the basis of his work as a retoucher (1964 and 1965).

From 1966 to 1967, Edy Brunner worked as a trainee industrial designer in Hans Kronenberg's studio in Lucerne. He later worked until 1968 as a graphic artist and designer for an advertising agency in Zürich and in Bruno Kessler's graphic studio in Maur near Zürich. He has been working freelance since December 1968.

Edy Brunner created his first kinetic and serial objects and multiples in 1967. That same year, together with Marc Kuhn, he had his first exhibition at the Galerie La Fourmière in Zürich. In 1968, he was awarded a grant by the Kiefer-Hablitzel Foun-

dation. In 1969, 1970 and 1971, he received the Swiss federal art grant.

In March/April 1969, Harald Szeemann organized an exhibition entitled "Wenn Attitüden Form werden. Werke – Konzepte – Vorgänge – Situationen – Information" at the Bern Kunsthalle. This exhibition brought together the very latest work in the field of conceptual art on a scale hitherto unparalleled in Europe. Like many other Swiss artists of his generation, Edy Brunner was profoundly influenced by this exhibition. He concentrated increasingly on conceptual art. His conceptual photo tableaux of 1969 to 1971 are amongst the most important works to have been created in this field. When the Swiss

Page 206 top left:
First solo exhibition, Galerie La Fourmière, Zürich, 1967
From left to right: Edy Brunner, Remo Galli, Marc Kuhn

Page 206 bottom left:
Incontro designer team, Bern, 1970
From left to right: Remo Galli, Edy Brunner, Thomas Kühne

Page 206 top right:
Edy Brunner with his "Apollo", 1970

Page 206 centre right:
Brunner's studio at the Istituto Svizzero, Rome, 1971/1972

Page 206 bottom right:
At the Istituto Svizzero, Rome, 1971/1972
From left to right: René Eisenegger, H. R. Ambauen, Prof. Gustav Ineichen, Bruno Gasser, Edy Brunner, Piero del Bondio, Theo Gerber, Renate Eisenegger

Page 207:
Exhibition at the Sigristen-Keller, Bülach, 1972

federal art commission adjudicated their awards in 1970, Brunner's "Apollo 11" tableau was at the centre of a heated debate on the classification and categorization of such work. Photography, until then, had been classified as applied art. Brunner's tableau was the first photographic work to qualify for a fine arts grant. In 1971, he received the grant for three further photo tableaux, again acknowledged as fine art.

Edy Brunner created his first major work as a designer in 1970, together with the architects Remo Galli and Thomas Kühne. Their interior design for the "Incontro" home decor store in Bern received considerable critical acclaim. Since 1970, he has been regularly commissioned to design trade fair stands for the American group of companies Dow Chemical Europe S.A., and until 1983 he worked closely with the designer Edgar Reinhard.

From 1971 to 1972, Edy Brunner had a grant allowing him to study at the Istituto Svizzero di Roma where he began to move away from individual art objects and towards social and ecological issues, which he sought to express primarily in art for public spaces. In the spring of 1972, he published the following statement in a documentation brochure issued by the Istituto Svizzero di Roma: *The works presented here date from the past five years. For me, living and working in Rome has been a kind of transition. My new plans are very differnt. I would like to be involved in housing projects, in designing an environment to live in, in planning the surroundings in which people of all ages live. I do not wish to present my art to the world in the form of individual works; I would like to make it accessible to the greatest possible number of people within a larger context of everyday life. In this respect, I regard art as a contribution towards life in the community.*

In the period that followed, Edy Brunner created major environments, fountains and projects for public spaces. For example, from 1972 to 1976, together with Karl Schneider, he was in charge of the artistic environmental design of the Zürich-Heuried housing project. Major fountains include his 1978 "Chempe Fountain" on the grounds of the VITA insurance

company in Zürich-Wieding and his 1984 "Molecular Fountain" at the head office of Serono S.A. in Aubonne.

In 1972, Brunner's most important solo exhibition of objects, multiples and conceptual photographs to date was held at the Sigristen-Keller in Bülach. The largest and most comprehensive exhibition of his photographic work was shown in 1991 at the Galerie Roter Turm in Halle an der Saale.

With his designs for eye-catching trade fair stands, for example at the plastics trade fair K '83, K '86 and K '89 in Düsseldorf, he set new standards for individual trade fair design and built up a reputation as one of the most interesting

Page 208 top left:
Edy Brunner and Edgar Reinhard with their truck at a trade fair in Paris, 1975

Page 208 top right:
Working on the "Chempe fountain" in Zürich-Wieding, 1980

Page 208 bottom right:
Working on a model of the "Molecular Fountain" at the Obere Zäune studio in Zürich, 1982

Page 209 top:
Building the "Molecular Fountain" in Aubonne, 1984

Page 209 left:
Working on the installation of the "Wasserspiegel" on the River Limmat in Zürich, 1986

Page 209 right:
With Markus Roth at the Obere Zäune studio in Zürich, 1988

Swiss exhibition designers. In 1991, he built the Swiss Pavilion for the international Telecom exhibition in Geneva, his largest design work in this field to date. In 1982, Edy Brunner began taking photographs with a panorama camera on his travels. The work he created soon achieved an artistic quality that allowed him to publish a selection of his photographs in his 1987 book "viewpoint". Between 1990 and 1991, he created the first major series of panorama photos at a single place over a lengthy period of time in Dresden. His book "Dresden" was published in 1993 by Edition Stemmle and was awarded the international Kodak Photo Book Prize the same year.

Page 210 top:
Working with Francesco Mariotti on the "Waterbirds", 1991

Page 210 bottom left:
Edy Brunner and Matthias Griebel, director of the Stadtmuseum Dresden, at the inauguration of the exhibition in Dresden on 11 September 1993

Page 210 bottom right:
Edy Brunner taking photographs, Entlebuch, 1991

Page 211 top:
With Willy Rotzler at the Einsiedlerstrasse studio in Wädenswil, 1993

Page 211 bottom left:
At the opening of the exhibition in the main building of the Alusuisse-Lonza Holding AG, Zürich, 1992
From left to right: Willy Rotzler, Edy Brunner, Axel Wendelberger, Christina Sitte

Page 211 bottom right:
With Walter Leuthold, Zürich, 1995

Exhibitions

Solo exhibitions

1967
Galerie La Fourmière, Zürich
(together with Marc Kuhn)

1968
Club Bel Etage, Zürich

1968
Galerie Brechbühl, Grenchen
(together with Willi Gutmann)

1969
Galerie Katakombe, Basel
(together with Jean Pfaff)

1972
Berner Galerie, Bern
(with Press-Art by Herbert Distel)

1989
Photoforum Pasquart, Biel

1989
Club der Kulturschaffenden J.R. Becher, Berlin (East)

1990
Galerie Roter Turm, Halle/Saale

1991
Photogalerie BILD, Baden

1992
Head office of Alusuisse-Lonza Holding AG, Zürich

1993
Stadtmuseum Dresden

1993
Galerie Michael Neumann, Düsseldorf

Group exhibitions

1967
Galerie Fritz Tschanz, Solothurn

1967
Galerie Aktuell, Bern

1967
Galerie Platte 27, Zürich

1969
Galerie Katakombe, Basel 1970 ART 70, Basel

1971
The Swiss Avant Garde, New York Cultural Center, New York

1971
4a BIENNALE DI BOLZANO, Bolzano

1971/1972
Photo Media, Museum of Contemporary Crafts, New York

1972
Idols, Aktionsgalerie Bern / Katakombe Basel / Bündner Kunsthaus

1973
Stadt in der Schweiz, Kunsthaus Zürich

1973
Tell 73, Helmhaus Zürich

1976
La Biennale di Venezia

1978
Das Schubladenmuseum, Kunsthaus Zürich
(and other museums in Europe and the USA)

1986
Mit erweitertem Auge – Berner Künstler und die Fotografie, Kunstmuseum Bern

Literature

Newspapers and periodicals

M. Hölzel: Edy Brunner und Marc Kuhn in der "Fourmière".
In: Volksrecht (Kunstspiegel), Winterthur, 23 November 1967

fbr. (Fritz Billeter): Gezielte und weniger gezielte Experimente.
In: Tages-Anzeiger, Zürich, 30 November 1967, p. 21

Lg.: Aufforderung zum (ernsten) Spiel. Zwei interessante
Gestalter stellen in der Galerie Brechbühl aus.
In: Grenchner Tagblatt, Grenchen, 10 May 1968, p. 47

E.F.: Junge Kunst auf alten und neuen Wegen. Stipendienausstellung 1968 der Kiefer-Hablitzel-Stiftung.
In: Luzerner Neueste Nachrichten, Luzern, 7 October 1968, p. 6

Willy Rotzler: Renaissance der Objekt-Kunst nach 1945.
In: du, Zürich, September 1969, p. 675

p.d.: Ein Kunststipendium für 24.000 Farbfotos. Edy Brunner
(Meilen) wurde für das "Dokumentationsbild Apollo 11" mit
dem Eidgenössischen Kunststipendium ausgezeichnet.
In: Zürichsee-Zeitung, 10 March 1970, p. 21"

"Apollo 11" – Dokumentationsbild mit dem Eidgenössischen
Kunststipendium ausgezeichnet.
In: Meilener Anzeiger, 13 March 1970

P.H. (Hans Peter Held): "Dokumentationsbild Apollo 11".
In: Ringiers Unterhaltungs-Blätter, Zofingen, 18 April 1970,
p. 50

M. Bruell/J. H. Bruell: Ein Ei geht auf Reisen.
In: Neue Zürcher Zeitung, Zürich, 17 May 1970, p. 62

Jürg H. Meyer: Ein Ei auf Herrn Kolumbus' Spuren.
In: Tages-Anzeiger, Zürich, 21 May 1970, p. 49

J.H.M. (Jürg H. Meyer): Das Mondlandeunternehmen Apollo 11
in 24.000 Farbfotos.
In: Tages-Anzeiger, Zürich, 14 July 1970, p. 15

Moderne Kunst in der IBM Schweiz.
In: IBM MOSAIC, Zürich, 1/March 1971 (10. Jg.), p. 10

shopping by ... incontro.
In: modernes wohnen. schweizer zeitschrift für internationales
wohnen. Zumikon, No. 41/71 (13. Jg., 1971), p. 29 ff.

GT: Der Uetiker Edy Brunner im Bülacher Sigristenkeller.
In: Zürichsee-Zeitung, 27 March 1972, p. 6

rs.: Im Bülacher Sigristenkeller: "Brunner kommt".
In: Tages-Anzeiger, 30 March 1972, p. 57

Leonardo Bezzola: "BRUNNER KAM".
In: werk, Zürich, 6/1972, p. 337 f.

z.: Wenn man sich Rosen schenkt – in Bern.
In: Der Bund, Bern, 13 October 1972, p. 43

pjb.: Berner Galerie: Press-Art und Edy Brunner.
In: Berner Tagblatt, 23 October 1972, p. 9

pm: Rationalisiertes Einkaufszentrum oder verträumte Boutique.
In: Raum + Handwerk, 2/1973

Hans Peter Held: Die Freiheit des Designers. Ausstellungskonzepte für Dow Chemical Europe S.A.
In: NOVUM Gebrauchsgraphik. Munich, 12 (December)/1973,
p. 18 ff.

Siedlung mit Gesicht.
In: Züri Leu, Zürich, 18 June 1976, p. 19

G.R.: Die Wohnsiedlungen Heuried und Utohof in Wiedikon.
In: Neue Zürcher Zeitung, Zürich, 22 June 1976

Wohnüberbauung Heuried in Zürich-Wiedikon.
In: werk / oeuvre, St. Gall, 12 / 1976, p. 828 ff.

Künstl. Schmuck VITA-Bürogebäude "Wieding". 1. Preis:
Edy Brunner.
In: Aktuelle Wettbewerbsszene. Schweizer Fachjournal für
Architektur und Baudesign, Zürich, 4/5, 1978, p. 109 ff.

D.D.: Wenn "Chempe" tanzen ... Neue Chancen für "Kunst
am Bau" beim VITA-Neubau Zürich Wieding.
In: Der Bund, Bern, 15 July 1978, p. 29

Das Interview. Heute mit Edy Brunner, Schöpfer von CHEMPE.
In: Blickpunkt Wieding 3. Zürich: VITA Versicherung, December 1978, p. 4 ff.

Breath of life.
In: International Herald Tribune, London, 4 April 1979, p. 4

Die Vita auf dem Wieding-Hügel.
In: Neue Zürcher Zeitung, Zürich, 13 November 1980, p. 49

Ein Felssturz in Wiedikon.
In: Tages-Anzeiger, Zürich, 14 November 1980, p. 19

Edy Brunner-Brunnen.
In: Zürich-Gazette, Zürich, 15 December 1980, p. 6

Dona Galli-Dejaco: Felssturz – und wie man einen macht.
In: Werk, Bauen + Wohnen, Zürich 4/1981, p. 6 f.

Franz Hohler: Brunners Steinschlag.
In: Weltwoche Magazin, Zürich, 5 August 1981 (No. 32),
p. 24 ff.

RDS: Mitten in Zürich: Steinschlag. Kaum ist der Platz fertig,
da geht einer hin und zertrümmert die Arbeit wieder.
In: Sonntags-Zeitung, Zürich, 23 August 1981, p. 5

Christoph Hackelsberger: Findlinge-Setzlinge. Ein lapidarer
Versuch künstlerischer Verfremdung.
In: Süddeutsche Zeitung, Stuttgart, 19/20 December 1981,
p. 87

HM: Edy Brunners "Chempe". "Chempe" d'Edy Brunner. Edy
Brunner's "Chempe".
In: anthos, Zürich, 2/1982, p. 9 ff.

(Leonardo Bezzola): Umgebungsgestaltung und Brunnenanlage in Aubonne VD.
In: anthos, Zürich, 4/1986, p. 19

(mf.): Spieglein, Spieglein in der Limmat ...
In: Zürifäscht. (Extrablatt). Zürich: Verkehrsverein, 1986, p. 2

(thas): Des Grossmünsters Grimassen in der Limmat.
In: Tages-Anzeiger, Zürich, 2 July 1986

(sda): Ein "Wasserspiegel" auf der Limmat.
In: Neue Zürcher Zeitung, Zürich, 3 July 1986, p. 46

(sda): Ein "Wasserspiegel" schwimmt auf der Limmat.
In: Neue Zürcher Zeitung, Zürich, 3 July 1986, p. 5

(c): 2000 Jahre Zürich spiegeln sich in der Limmat.
In: Zürichsee-Zeitung, Zürich, 3 July 1986, p. 7

Willy Rotzler: 25 Jahre Kunst in der Schweiz.
In: das kunstwerk, Stuttgart, 4/5 (September)/1986, p. 28

Peter Pachnicke: Berückende und rätselhafte Fremdheit.
In: Neue Berliner Illustrierte, East Berlin, No. 28/1989, p. 23

Hans-Georg Sehrt: Fotos aus dem Plaste-Ei. Edy-Brunner-
Ausstellung in der Galerie Roter Turm.
In: Mitteldeutsche Neueste Nachrichten, Halle, 7 May 1990

Hans-Georg Sehrt: Eigenwilliges eines Schweizer Fotografen.
In: Mitteldeutsche Zeitung, Halle, 10 April 1990, p. 5

F. Reinke: Die Faszination der Stille.
In: Tribüne, Eas Berlin, 17 April 1990

Peter H. Blattmann: Wie es zu unserer Stelze kam.
In: häsch g'hört. Zeitschrift für die Betriebsangehörigen von
Blattmann+CoAG, Wädenswil, No. 69/Winter 1991, p. 36 ff.

Christina Sitte: Sehen, Erkennen, Photographieren. Beachtenswertes Kunstschaffen in den Kleinstädten.
In: Die Synthese, Zürich, No. 239/December 1991, p. 11

Walter Stampa: Edy Brunner, Künstler und Gestalter.
In: EXPO DATA, Zürich, 4 (April)/1992, p. 24 ff.

24. Internationaler Fotokalender-Preis.
In: PROFIFOTO, Düsseldorf, 2 (March/April)/1993, p. 49 ff.

Genia Bleier: Ein Schweizer entdeckt Dresden.
In: Dresdener Neueste Nachrichten, 11/12 September 1993

Konrad Hirsch: Dresden zwischen Verharren und Hoffnung.
Panoramafotografien von Edy Brunner im Stadtmuseum.
In: Dresdener Neueste Nachrichten, 14 September 1993

Klaus Sebastian: Jagdschlösser, stille Elbdampfer und Trabis.
In: Rheinische Post, No. 13

MGM: Spaziergänge mit der Kamera. Dresden – aus der Sicht
des Fotokünstlers Edy Brunner.
In: Neue Rhein-Zeitung, 15 January 1994

Exhibition catalogues and books

Edy Brunner. Marc Kuhn (Exhibition catalogue).
Zürich: Galerie La Fourmière, 1967

BRUNNER GUTMANN BEI GALERIE BRECHBÜHL GRENCHEN.
(Exhibition catalogue). Grenchen: Galerie Brechbühl, 1968

The Swiss Avant Garde. (Exhibition catalogue).
New York: New York Cultural Center, 1971, p. 86 f.

4a BIENNALE DI BOLZANO. (Exhibition catalogue).
Bolzano, 1971, p. 152 f.

Walter Aue: P.C.A. Projecte, Concepte & Actionen.
Cologne: Verlag DuMont Schauberg, 1971

Gerhard Johann Lischka (ed.): Idols. (Exhibition catalogue).
Bern: Walter Zürcher Verlag, 1972, p. 9

Gustav Ineichen (ed.): AMBAUEN. BRUNNER. DEL BONDIO.
EISENEGGER. GASSER. GERBER.
Rome: Istituto Svizzero di Roma, 1971/72

Willy Rotzler: OBJEKTE-KUNST. Von Duchamp bis Kienholz.
Cologne: Verlag DuMont Schauberg, 1972, p. 186

Wolfgang Grub: Boutiquen, Shops und schicke Läden. Internationale Beispiele verkaufsfördernd gestaltet.
Munich: Verlag Georg D.W. Callwey, 1974, p. 48 f. p. 64 f.

Schweiz. Suisse. Svizzera. 37. Biennale di Venezia 1976.
(Exhibition catalogue). Zürich: Eidgenössisches Amt für kulturelle Angelegenheiten, 1976

La Biennale di Venezia 1976. Environment, Participation, Cul-
tural Structures. General Catalogue. First Volume.
(Exhibition catalogue). Venice: Edizioni "LA BIENNALE DI
VENEZIA", 1976, p. 144 ff.

Jean-Luc Daval (ed.): ART ACTUEL. SKIRA ANNUEL No. 3.
Geneva: Editions Skira et Cosmopress, 1977, p. 102

Herbert Distel: Das Schubladenmuseum. Le musée en tiroirs.
The Museum of Drawers. (Exhibition catalogue).
Zürich: Kunsthaus, 1978, p. 23, 39

Wohnsiedlungen Heuried und Utohof Zürich-Wiedikon.
Zürich: Stadt Zürich, September 1978

Karl and Eva Mang: Neue Läden.
Stuttgart: Verlag Gerd Hatje, 1981, p. 114 f.

DOW DREIUNDACHTZIG. (Exhibition catalogue).
Horgen: Dow Chemical Europe, 1983

Rolf H. Krauss / Manfred Schmalriede / Michael Schwarz:
Kunst mit Photographie. Die Sammlung Dr. Rolf H. Krauss.
(Exhibition catalogue). Berlin: Verlag Fröhlich & Kaufmann,
1983, p. 106 f., p. 323

Rolf Lambrigger: Zürich. Zeitgenössische Kunstwerke im Frei-
en. Zürich/Schwäbisch Hall: Orell Füssli Verlag, 1985, p. 256 f.

Stefan Frey (ed.): Mit erweitertem Auge. Berner Künstler
und die Fotografie. (Exhibition catalogue).
Bern: Bernische Stiftung für Fotografie, Film und Video (FFV)/
Benteli Verlag, 1986, p. 105 f., 154, 228 f.

Edy Brunner: viewpoint. (With a foreword by Willy Rotzler and
essays by Franz Hohler. German and English).
Zürich: ABC-Verlag, 1987

Urs Stahel / Martin Heller: Fotografie in der Schweiz. Wichtige
Bilder. (Exhibition catalogue). Zürich: Der Alltag / Museum für
Gestaltung, 1990, p. 170, 178, 190

Peter and Ruth Fenkart (ed.): Halbzeit. Fünfzig 50jährige zur
Schweiz. Zürich: Werd Verlag, 1993

Dresden. Panoramafotografien von Edy Brunner. (Calendar
1993. With a text by Axel Wendelberger. In German).
Ditzingen and Gotha: Grafisches Zentrum Drucktechnik, 1992

DRESDEN. Panoramafotografien 1990/91 von Edy Brunner.
(With a foreword by Matthias Griebel and an essay by Axel
Wendelberger. In German).
Schaffhausen: Edition Stemmle, 1993

DRESDEN. Panoramafotografien 1990/91. (Portfolio of 30
original photographs by Edy Brunner. Accompanying text by
Grit Wendelberger. In German).
Düsseldorf: Galerie Neumann, 1993

Willy Rotzler: Edy Brunner. Die Gabe zum Sehen. 1987. In:
ders.: Aus dem Tag in der Zeit. Texte zur modernen Kunst.
Zürich: Offizin Zürich Verlags AG, 1994

Colophon

© 1995 Edy Brunner

Editor:
Sabine Dausend, Wuppertal

Translation:
Ishbel Flett
Cathy Ziegler (pages 7, 99)

Design and Layout:
Axel Wendelberger and Edy Brunner

Typography:
Axel Wendelberger

Photo credits:
Leonardo Bezzola, Lorenzo Bianda, Edy Brunner, Klaus E.
Göltz, Christian Känzig, Bruno Lienhard, F. Meyer-Henn,
Christina Sitte, Susanne Trappmann, Van der Rejken, Ernst
Vogelsanger, E. T. Werlen, Archive Edy Brunner

Computer animation:
Walter Leuthold, Zürich

Lithography:
Lanarepro GmbH, Lana/Italy
Neidhart + Schön AG, Zürich/Switzerland

Printed by:
Neidhart + Schön AG, Zürich/Switzerland

Bound by:
Buchbinderei Burkhart, Mönchaltorf/Switzerland

Edition Stemmle, Kilchberg-Zürich/Switzerland

English Edition:
ISBN 3-905514-90-7

German Edition:
ISBN 3-905514-48-6

This book has been published with the kind support of the
Swiss cultural foundation Pro Helvetia.

Printed in Switzerland